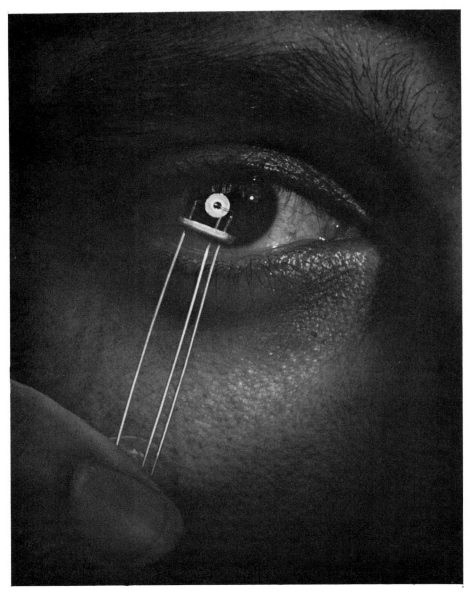

1. Transistor Element, Eye. Made with Hasselblad Camera and 80mm lens with extension tube, and one light in a cone reflector. The shadows were illuminated from environmental light in the laboratory, and placed on Zones I and II. Emphasis is on the transistor element; the light was turned slightly away from the plane of the eye (using only the edge of the field of illumination), which gave full illumination to the principal subject. A piece of cardboard was held in front of the reflector so as to cut off the light falling on the thumb; being held close to the reflector, it produced a broad shadow and a soft transition from light to dark. Close subjects of this character demand very careful positioning of the camera and lights, and a precise determination of exposure. In this case approximately 1.6x normal exposure was required because of the extension of the lens beyond "infinity" focus position.

ARTIFICIAL-LIGHT

PHOTOGRAPHY

ANSEL ADAMS

Basic Photo 5

NEW YORK GRAPHIC SOCIETY • BOSTON

FOREWORD

"Let the eyes work from inside out"

Edward Weston

I dedicate these books to everyone who is interested in the development of straightforward photography and who believes in the simple statement of the lens.

I extend my appreciation to my many friends and associates who have helped so generously in the preparation of this book. I wish to thank the International Business Machines Corporation for their kind permission to use the pictures represented in plates 1, 8, 21, 38 and 45, and the University of Rochester, Rochester, New York, for the use of pictures represented in plates 4, 6, 22, 23, 24, 26 and 47. Other credits are given in the picture captions.

Serving as Consultant in Photography for the Polaroid Corporation, I have had the privilege of testing in the field many of the new materials and equipment prototypes, and I am deeply grateful for their cooperation in permitting use of some of the new materials for illustrations in this book.

International Standard Book Number: 0-8212-0720-2
Library of Congress Catalog Card Number: 76-53281

New York Graphic Society books are published by Little, Brown and Company. Published simultaneously in Canada by Little, Brown and Company (Canada) Limited

Published in the United States of America
HOR

Light, to the accomplished photographer, is as much an actuality as substance like rock or flesh; it is an element to be evaluated and interpreted. The *impression* of light and the *impression* of substance which are achieved through careful use of light are equally essential to the realistic photographic image. Light may be used as the dominant element in expressive photography, where "departure from reality," or emotional and aesthetic emphasis, are desired. While much of the best contemporary photography has been accomplished with natural light, we must recognize the fact that artificial light can be a powerful creative tool. Much emphasis is directed to purely mechanical and spectacular effects without awareness of the basic aesthetic potentials and qualities of light artificially produced and directed upon the subject.

A distinction must be made here between the terms "natural light" and "artificial light." To me, "natural light" means any illumination that is not completely manipulated or obviously controlled—daylight, daylight through windows, firelight, and light from existing fixtures in normal use. Perhaps a better term for "natural light" would be "existing light." (The term "available light" is often used.) For example, I enter a room and find a person reading by a table lamp. I simply select the most desirable point of view and photograph the person as I find him. I may use a mild amount of reflected light to "boost" otherwise uncontrolled shadow values; but I take care that this control will not be obvious in the finished picture.

In my use of the term, the picture has been made by "existing light"; I have not altered the position or intensity of the light source, or conceived my composition chiefly in terms of light controls. If I have raised the shadow values by adding more light *of the same quality*, I have not violated the principle as stated. But if I use one or more floodlights, flashlamps or strong reflectors, and arbitrarily direct both lighting and subject under the imposed light, I would consider the lighting *artificial*. Throughout this volume the emphasis is on artificial and controlled lighting, although "synchro-sunlight" and combination of natural and artificial light will be discussed.

Artificial light should not be thought of as an *imitation* of natural light. With natural light, only minor controls of the light itself are possible by the use of screens and reflectors, and by selection of viewpoint. With artificial light the photographer can make striking modifications of appearances; in fact, he may create entirely new aspects of the subject before him.

In this book I shall not discuss many specific applications of artificial light in the professional fields. The highly developed aspects of fashion, commercial portraiture and industrial photography are literally worlds in themselves; they require relatively complex equipment and procedures and a wide experience in the *subjects* involved. Rather, I choose to set forth some principles which I consider basic in technical and expressive photography, and I am quite certain that the ambitious and capable photographer can carry on without difficulty in whatever branch of the art he may choose to follow. Those anticipating a conventional book on the subject will be disappointed; hundreds of such works exist on artificial light, and there is little reason to duplicate them. I find that the entire subject of artificial lighting has been molded into rigid patterns of procedure, mechanics and equipment, and it is my intention to approach the problems on a tangent of fresh concepts and relative simplicity.

The Previous Basic Photo Books

The function of this series of BASIC PHOTO BOOKS is to present a philosophy of technique and application. Every example and statement is set forth with the hope that the photographer and the serious student will use it as the basis for personal experiment and for the development of a *personal* approach to the art of the camera.

Photography, in the final analysis, can be reduced to a few simple principles. But, unlike most arts, it seems complex at the initial approach. The seeming complexity can never be resolved unless a fundamental understanding of both techniques and application is sought and exercised from the start.

Photography is more than a medium for factual communication of ideas. It is a creative art. Therefore emphasis on technique is justified only insofar as it will simplify and clarify the statement of the photographer's concept. My object is to present a working technique for creative photography.

Books 1, 2, and 3 are basically technical in character and explore the controls and disciplines that I believe are essential to a good command of the craft of photography. Book 4 explored some of the possibilities of applied photography in natural light, and, together with Book 5, recapitulates some of the technical expositions of the first three books. The scope and possibilities of photography are so vast that it would be ridiculous to suggest that any approach is the "final" one or contains the full measure of the technical and expressive potentials of the medium.

The Personal Approach

My basic approach to photography depends on visualization of the final print before the exposure is made. When the print is conceived in the mind, either as a realistic statement or as an intentional "departure from reality," the brightness values of the subject are determined (by careful exposure-meter readings) and are placed appropriately on the exposure scale. The negative is exposed and developed for the desired rendition. The print from such a negative requires a minimum of development control, dodging or use of extreme paper contrast grades. This procedure is not only efficient, but also gives the photographer control of his craft at all times, and the assurance of satisfactory results. With practice—following careful experimentation and full understanding of the equipment used—this method becomes quite automatic.

The purpose of this approach is to *simplify* technique, to give the individual a command of his own interpretive style, and to encompass a wide variety of photographic problems. It is the opposite of the empirical method, in which, by a long process of trial and error, the photographer "finds out" the most effective ways and means to achieve his ends. My approach requires a serious attitude toward photography and the willingness to spend considerable time and energy in basic studies. In this, however, photography in no way differs from any other serious art and craft; the end result of this attitude, and the willingness to study and experiment, is a greater freedom and spontaniety in actual practice.

We may draw an analogy to music. The composer entertains a musical idea. He sets it down in conventional musical notation. When he performs it he may, although respecting the score, apply personal expressive interpretations to the basic structure of the notes. So it is in expressive photography. The concept of the photography precedes the operation of the camera. Exposure and development of the negative follow technical patterns selected to achieve the qualities desired in the final print, and the print itself is virtually an *interpretation*—a *performance* of the photographic idea.

It must be clearly understood by everyone that the philosophy and the approach set forth in this book (and in the other books of the series) are definitely those of Ansel Adams; and that while there is no deviation from basic principles, of course, some terminology and the inclusion of expressive factors may differ in a number of instances from conventional photographic terminology and practical procedures. Such deviations are the logical outgrowth of considerable experience in professional work and teaching. It is my firm conviction that a useful bridge has never been constructed between practical creative work and the scientific aspects of sensitometry. This book sets forth a working procedure based on my personal methods, which have a fluid and adaptable approach rather than a rigid pattern, and are subject to continuous expansion and clarification.

The recent advances in the Polaroid Land Process open new vistas for functional and expressive photography. Not only does the process serve to "check" lighting, exposure and composition in conventional photography, but — and more important — it is in itself a new creative medium. Not only are the images of exceptional scale and beauty of tone, but they lend themselves to direct enlarged reproduction by means of letterpress, lithography and gravure, as well as by photocopying. The resolution of the new materials, especially of the Type 55 P/N Polaroid Land Film Packets, Types 52 and 51 (high-contrast material), and Types 46L and 146L Transparency Film, is very high, and have many professional applications. Since the earlier editions of this book, the Type 100 cameras and packs have been developed (Type 107, 3000 speed, and Type 108, Polacolor). The Polaroid Land process and its applications are discussed at various points in this book, and a number of illustrations are direct engravings from the original Polaroid Land prints.

DESCRIPTION OF TERMS USED IN THIS BOOK

Although it is advisable that the reader have some basic knowledge of photographic technique and terminology as set forth in the preceding volumes of this series, it will be helpful to redefine here some terms frequently used in the following pages of this book.

Intensity: the degree of illumination from sun, sky, artificial light sources and reflectors; the amount of light falling *on* the subject as distinguished from the light reflected by it. Incident light is evaluated in terms of *intensity* (footcandles).

Brightness: the degree of light reflected *from* the subject to the eye, meter, lens and film. Reflected light is evaluated in terms of *Luminance*. Luminance values herein are given in *candles per square foot* (c/ft^2), which are the units of measurement of the Weston Meter. Other terms, such as *footlambert*, also relate to luminance values, and conversion of c/ft^2 units is relatively simple: $Ft.L/\pi = c/ft^2$. **NOTE:** Since the last printing of this book, I have favored the use of the term Luminance instead of Brightness as conveying a more logical meaning of the qualities of reflected light. Please substitute the word Luminance for Brightness throughout the book.

Opacity or Density: A quality of the developed negative image. Either term expresses the same value—*opacity* in arithmetical terms, *density* in logarithmic terms. *Opacity* is used frequently in these books; it can be understood more readily by readers not mathematically inclined. It refers directly to the light-stopping powers of the negative.

Brilliancy: This relates to the amount of light reflected from the finished print (hence related to the visual contrast of the print image). Brilliancy is modified by the color or tone of the print image, and the surface characteristics of the paper, as well as by the quality and intensity of the light under which the print is viewed. Brilliancy is the arithmetical equivalent of *reflection density.*

Gray Card: A surface of paper or painted material which reflects "neutral" gray (light without domination of any color). With the Kodak Neutral Test Card the reflectance of the gray side is about 18 per cent, and the white side is about 90 per cent. The gray side represents "middle gray" (Zone V) and the white side (under the same illumination) represents a point on the exposure scale between Zones VII and VIII. In sunlight the gray side approximates the brightness of the clear blue sky (200 c/ft^2) with the surface of the gray card at about 45° to the sun. If this value (200 c/ft^2) is placed on Zone V, Zone I will represent a brightness of 13 c/ft^2, and Zone VIII will represent 1,600 c/ft^2. This suggests the exposure range of the negative material in reference to the brightness range of the subject. When purely mechanical reproduction of values is required, the gray card will be helpful. The intensity of artificial lighting can be controlled by reference to the comparative brightness of the gray card at different positions on the subject.

Filter Exposure Factor: A factor indicating the amount of increase of exposure required when a filter is used. This factor depends upon the character of the negative material and the color quality of the light, and to a certain extent on the color quality of the subject. The published factors for various filters and negative materials are based on "daylight" and "tungsten" light as reflected from a neutral gray surface. Refer to page 3 for more extensive description.

Lens Extension Factor: When lenses are focused on near objects they are extended beyond the infinity-focus position, and the ratio of lens stop to focal length becomes less; the lens thereby transmits less light to the film. For example, with an 8-inch lens at infinity focus, f/16 is represented by a stop 1/2-inch in diameter. If the lens is extended to a little over 11 inches, this 1/2-inch aperture becomes f/22, thereby requiring 2x normal exposure. The formula is simple:

$$\frac{(\text{Measured Lens Extension})^2}{(\text{Nominal Focal Length})^2} = \text{Exposure Factor}$$

$$\frac{(11.2)^2}{(8)^2} = \frac{125}{64} = 2x$$

Except for exceptionally critical work, extension factors of less than 1.25 may be disregarded. A simple dial guide, the Kodak Effective Aperture Computer, will give the correct lens stop for those not mathematically inclined.

viii

Flash Exposure Factor (Guide Number): A factor experimentally determined to correlate film sensitivity, lens stop and shutter speed, lamp-to-subject distance, speedlight and flashlamp intensity. Guide numbers can also be determined for photoflood and other sources. The formulas for the guide numbers (distance in feet) are:

Guide number = Lens Stop x Distance of Lamp from Subject (in feet)

Distance of Lamp from Subject = Guide Number ÷ Lens Stop

Lens Stop Used = Guide Number ÷ Distance of Lamp from Subject

The ratio is geometric: double the Guide Number represents 4x the light intensity, etc. Factors are modified by reflectors, shutter speeds, environmental effects, etc.

Incident Light: See *Intensity.*

Reflected Light: See *Brightness.*

Reciprocity Effect: Commonly called the *failure of the reciprocity law.* The reciprocity law: $E = It$. In theory, 100 units of light with 1/100-second exposure should give the same negative density as 1 unit of light with 1-second exposure. This holds for normal exposure, but very long or very short exposures yield abnormal results, and compensation must be made by increasing exposure on one hand, and development on the other. The reciprocity effect is mentioned frequently in this book. See page 4.

Lighting Terms

Core: That part of the subject which does not receive direct illumination from the principal light sources; for example, a portrait lighted by two lights, each behind the plane of the subject, will present an area of low or no illumination toward the lens. The brightness of the core can be controlled by general environmental or reflected light. See Fig. 50, page 92.

Steady-Burning Lights: Lights such as tungsten lamps or photofloods, fluorescent lamps, etc., which burn constantly during the exposure; in contradistinction to:

Flashlamps: Providing illumination of short duration which can be fully or partially used, depending upon the shutter speeds; and

Speedlamps: Electronic discharge lamps of extremely short duration (much shorter than any standard shutter speed available).

Modeling Lights: Lights which are used to compose and balance brightnesses; used prior to exposure by flashlamps and speedlamps. They are so placed that they represent the identical direction and quality of illumination derived from the flashlamps and speedlamps. They should be of relatively low intensity—at least during the actual flash exposure—in order to avoid any secondary image effects. A rheostat control can be attached to the modeling light circuit which will reduce the lights from normal intensity to the desired low intensity at the moment of exposure.

Reflectors: Devices in which the various lamps are placed and which influence the quality and intensity of the light.

Reflecting Screens: Reflecting surfaces of fabric, cardboard, wood or plastic, which are usually painted white and are used to reflect light onto otherwise non-illuminated areas. These can be called *screens*—but they should not be confused with the diffusing screens which are sometimes used between the lamps and the subject to modify the quality of the light.

Axis Light: Light which is directed to the subject from a source on or very close to the axis of the lens (which is perpendicular to the plane of the negative).

Main Light: The principal light source.

Second Light: The next important light; it may be direct light or reflected light.

Decorative Light: A light used to accent a part of the subject; such as a light above a portrait subject, placed to put a gleam on the hair.

Environmental Light: Light falling upon the subject from reflecting surfaces of the environment (walls, ceiling, clothing, etc.) which may or may not appear in the field of view. It augments the general brightness of the subject, and therefore affects both contrast and exposure values.

Bounced Light: Light from any source which is directed *to* a reflecting surface and therefrom illuminates the subject. This might be confused with ordinary reflected light, except that it is used mostly in the sense of its being a principal source of illumination. Also, it usually reflects light from a separate lamp, and not from the main lamp only. See page 43.

Spotlight: A light collimated by optical means, usually of restricted field and high intensity.

Polarization: The control of reflections is achieved by use of the polarizers, just as with natural light. The effect of these devices can be judged visually prior to exposure. See page 77.

The Photo Dictionary (Morgan & Morgan) offers a very comprehensive terminology of photo words and definitions.

Color photography is mentioned infrequently in this book; while the basic principles of photography apply to all phases of the medium, the specific techniques of color photography are very complex and cannot be adequately presented here. However, while the techniques are rapidly improving and becoming more flexible, they do not as yet match the elastic controls enjoyed with black-and-white photography.

NOTE: This is not a "picture book"; some images are included to *show* certain errors of plan or operation, or demonstrate a basic approach, and these are discussed in the picture captions or in the text.

It is difficult, if not impossible, to significantly demonstrate a particular operational situation; while countless problems confront the photographer, they are always integrated into the general technical and expressive objectives and may be hard to isolate for demonstration.

However, if the photographer *recognizes* these problems, and considers them as he plans and executes his picture, he will master most of them. Experience is a fine teacher, but experience alone is a time-consuming method of learning! Familiarity with operating conditions gives the photographer a considerable facility, but on the other hand he must guard against "pot-boiling" and sterile repetition of formula and effect.

It is important that the reader study Book 2 (The Negative); the exposition of the Zone System therein will prepare him for a better understanding of much of the informative material in this volume. Space does not permit a thorough recapitulation of the Zone System in this book.

TABLE OF CONTENTS

Illustrations and Diagrams

2. Charles Boyer (by Philippe Halsman). This beautiful portrait was made with a standard Rolleiflex, using one flashlamp held over the subject's head. It represents the utmost simplicity of technique and approach, and the results present poetic intensity and appropriate mood. Tungsten light, photoflood, or speedlight could all have been used with approximately the same effect. In studying this image we observe a sharply defined shadow edge and a rather compact highlight area, indicating that the light source was small in area (subtended a small angle; see page 16). At the same distance the light in large diffuse reflector would have produced a quite different effect, creating broad highlights, soft shadow edges, and a reduction in "textural" effect.

It is obvious there is little or no environmental light—the shadows are quite "empty." The shadow on the nose is slightly "boosted" by light reflected from the cheek. The exposure given was such that the shadows fell on, or below, threshold (Zone I). Textures are beautifully held in all illuminated areas. The absence of catchlights in the eyes accentuates the mask-like effect, which is further emphasized by the lack of environmental detail.

QUALITIES OF ARTIFICIAL LIGHT

Our impressions of the external world are chiefly tactile and visual, condi tioned by the experience of countless generations of organisms from the amœba to man. The qualities of natural light are as "inevitable" as the stones of the hills: intensity and direction of light are basic to any visual appreciation of objed and environment. By "natural light" I mean daylight (sunlight and skylight) and others forms of "existing" light. In Book 4 of this series, NATURAL-LIGHT PHOTOG RAPHY, I made a broad definition of natural and artificial light, and included the terms "existing" and "available" in relation to light "as we find it," opposed to "contrived" light or "as we create and control it." But such broad terms do not adequately describe light in its many forms as it applies to the problems of creative photography. We are as much concerned with the æsthetic and interpretive as with the physical and technical aspects of the art— and *appropriate* light (from any source) is the important element to consider. Hence I believe we may reduce the problem to two basic channels of approach: the world as seen by natural, unmodified light, and the world as interpreted by contrived and controlled light. The basic differences of these two approaches must be apparent to all who think about them.

We can say that sunlight, directed by mirrors on the subject with definite compositional intention, might be thought of as artificial or "contrived" light, and light from a fixed street lamp thought of as "natural" or "existing" light. To some readers such distinctions may appear precious and unnecessary, but I firmly believe they are in the basic æsthetic structure of creative photography. No questions of right or wrong, of good or bad, of art and non-art are implied. The whole concept of creative photography depends upon a logic of concept and approach, and light —as the prime tool of the photographer—deserves full consideration.

I wish to make it very clear at this point that I am not interested in the elaborate lighting procedures frequently applied in the professional photographic fields. I have before me an example of commercial work in which *eleven* lights are used—and the result is neither adequately revealing nor expressive. I feel that a simple approach to lighting—using the minimum of light sources—favors a convincing reality. I do not say it is *wrong* to use multiple lights; rather I feel it is usually quite unnecessary. It is not logical that the photograph stress the *lighting* more than the *subject*. This emphasis is frequently obvious in motion pictures, but also appears in much commercial and portrait work. On occasion, intentional dramatic effects may demand multiple lighting for strong contrasts, intricate highlight and shadow effects, and adequate illumination of complex subjects. I believe that the photographer—and especially the student—should approach the problem of artificial light with the utmost caution and restraint. The purpose of this book is not to describe conventional lighting techniques, but to explore the logical uses of artificial light so that the photographer will be encouraged to develop his own personal approach.

Types of Artificial Light

We have many sources of illumination at our command, such as arc lights, tungsten lamps, flashlamps, mercury lamps and fluorescent lamps. For the first three, which represent light of continuous spectra, definite color temperatures can be established ($°K$). For the remaining two, which represent light of discontinuous

1

spectra, we can only *approximate* color temperatures. Color photography with the second group becomes difficult; even with special compensating filters it is not possible to render colors as accurately as with daylight or tungsten lamps.

With black-and-white photography there is a relatively slight difference between the two types of light—except that the second type, usually produced by comparatively large areas of tubes and grids, gives "broader" illumination (softer highlights and shadow edges). We are therefore concerned with the intensity and quality of illumination—and of course with the obvious *color* of the light (strong reds, blues, or green lights)—not with the rather subtle differences expressed by *color temperatures.*

The *quality* of illumination refers to the following: even or uneven illumination over a given field; and the sharp or diffuse nature of the source. We know that a small source of light, such as an electric arc, will cast sharp shadows and create sharp highlights, while light from a bank of fluorescent tubes will give very soft shadows and broad highlights. The greater the angle subtended by the light source, the "softer" the illumination.

As the voltage drops, the light output lessens and the color temperature decreases (becomes "redder"). Photoflood lights are designed to give a high emission of light at normal voltages, but of course have a much longer life if operated at lower than normal voltages. Therefore, when *composing* with photofloods it is suggested that a voltage-reduction transformer be employed in the circuits. A switch of the "Hi-Low" type is recommended.

Fluorescent lamps will not operate except at near-standard voltages.

Flashlamps will fire from either battery or line circuits except when operated through synchronized shutters—in which case, to avoid serious damage to the shutter, only battery current should be used.

Speedlights (electronic flash) are very important in the domain of artificial illumination, and their use will be discussed on page 41 in considerable detail. They are rather complicated devices, and, because of the high voltages involved, certain safety precautions must be observed. Speedlight illumination is of high color temperature (6,000-7,000°K, about the same as daylight), and the light output is of very short duration, (about 1/700 to 1/1000 second for the average equipment).

Relative Film Speeds

Different film speeds for, say, a panchromatic film in daylight and in tungsten light are explained by the fact that, as the panchromatic film is sensitive to light of all colors, it is capable of maximum response to daylight (which contains red, green, yellow, blue and violet light). Now, as tungsten light is weak in the blue end of the spectrum, the general response of the film will be higher with daylight (in relation to the total intensity of illumination) than with tungsten light (roughly 3/4 daylight rating). Orthochromatic film, having no sensitivity to red light, is relatively more sensitive to green and blue light. But as tungsten light has a low output of blue light, the relative tungsten speed of orthochromatic film is proportionally low—usually about 1/2 that for daylight. (Refer to manufacturers' data sheets for exact film speeds.) A similar difference in effective speeds will be noticed at sunset when the sunlight is far "warmer" (more yellow) than in the earlier hours of the day.

Filter factors (exposure factors) are supposed to compensate for the use of color filters with standard illumination. However, when using filtered light of one color—red, green or blue—the actual contrast of the image varies; it is highest with red, moderate with green, and less with blue light. Hence, to achieve normal contrast with images made with monochromatic filters, we must develop less for red, a little more for green, and definitely more than normal for blue. (By "normal" we mean the "normal" development time for a negative made under ordinary, full spectrum illumination.) Ordinary yellow filters such as the K1, K2, No. 12 (minus blue), etc., while changing color values to a moderate extent (clearing atmospheric haze, etc., in natural light), have little effect on basic negative contrast.

It is not only that the negative emulsion *responds* differently to different colors, but also that the scattering of light *within* the emulsion affects the contrast. Red light scatters least, and therefore penetrates most. (Hence the need for reduced developing time to achieve optimum contrast under red light or when using a red filter). Blue light scatters most, and therefore penetrates least. (Hence the need for increased developing time to achieve optimum contrast under blue light or when using a blue filter.) * Exceptions: with modern thin-emulsion films and Polaroid Land films, there is little change in the *contrast* effects with various color filters.

As tungsten light contains more yellow, orange and red light, and less blue light than daylight, the exposure factors for the yellow, orange and red filters are less with tungsten light than with daylight.

Due to the relatively high proportion of yellow and red light in artificial illumination, some filter control will be required, especially in portraiture. With panchromatic film and *daylight*, red lips photograph rather light; with *tungsten light* the lips photograph *very* light (thus the need for "panchromatic" makeup —a magenta color for lips, etc.). With some high red-sensitive films lips photograph almost white. A light blue or ortho green filter such as the X1 will "'correct" the lip tone in daylight, but a stronger filter, such as an X2, will be required for tungsten light.

Other factors to consider when using artificial light are:

Inverse Square Law: The intensity of the light diminishes as the square of the distance (light source to subject) increases. See Figure 3, page 5.

For all practical purposes, there is no Inverse Square Law problem with daylight (except when using light from windows, skylights, reflecting screens, etc., considered as light sources), but with artificial light at the ordinary working distances a slight increase or decrease of light-to-subject may make a marked difference in the effective brightness values of the subject. For example, suppose we are working with an object about 4 feet long. Our light is placed about 5 feet from one end of the subject. The distance of the light from the other end would be about 9 feet. The ratio of brightness is therefore $5^2:9^2$, or 25:81—a difference of approxi-

---

*To demonstrate the scattering of light of different colors, merely project a spotlight or light from a film projector on a white surface in a darkened room. Place a red filter over the light and observe the amount of red light scattered throughout the room. Now place a blue filter over the light; much more blue light than red light will be scattered. Blue light scatters in the air, hence the blue of the sky. It also scatters in the emulsion of the film, and the more scatter, the less penetration and the less density of the negative for any given amount of exposure and development.

mately 1:3! Our visual mechanism compensates for these differences of illumination, and judgment based on visual impressions may often be seriously in error.

Environmental effects: Complex reflections which obey the Inverse Square Law and are often difficult to evaluate by the eye. Hence the need for a sensitive brightness meter.

Direction of Light: Specular (mirror-like) and diffuse reflectivities of the subject must not be overlooked; they may vary in relation to the direction of light falling upon them, and they must be evaluated from *camera position* only.

Reciprocity Effect: I am appreciative of the following practical information on the reciprocity effect as provided by Messrs. William Quandt and Pirkle Jones of the Photography Department of the California School of Fine Arts, San Francisco. The findings relate to Kodak Super-XX sheet film and may vary with other negative materials in common use. It is a relatively simple matter to test for the reciprocity effect by making comparative exposures. (Refer to page 59, Book 2, THE NEGATIVE. Also refer to Kodak Pamphlet No. O-2, *Reciprocity Data, Kodak Professional Black and White Films.*)

As discussed above, the reciprocity effect alters the *lower* tones of the scale first; hence the contrast scale of the negative is increased, and less development is indicated to maintain the same total opacity range. The degree of reduced development can be determined by calculating the effective position of the high values on the exposure scale; for example, if the calculated exposure were 32 seconds, and the reciprocity factor 4x, the higher values would fall about 2 zones higher on the scale, and the development time would be reduced accordingly (at least *normal-minus-one*, perhaps *normal-minus-two*), depending upon the position of the high values on the scale to begin with. In such cases the 2-solution developer (D-23 and 1 percent Borax) will be helpful in giving optimum density to the low values of the scale. See page 8.

Remember, the reciprocity effect depends upon the *length of exposure* (exposure time) *and is independent of illumination intensity, brightness of object photographed, lens stop used, etc.*

The exposure factors listed below are *approximate*, but quite satisfactory for practical work in black-and-white photography. The reciprocity effect in color photography presents a much more complex problem.

If the calculated exposure is: Increase exposure as follows:

4 seconds	use 1.5x or 6 seconds and 10% less development
8 seconds	use 2x or 16 seconds and 20% less development
16 seconds	use 2.5x or 40 seconds and 20% less development
32 seconds	use 3x or 96 seconds and 25% less development
64 seconds	use 4x or 256 seconds and 25% less development
100 seconds	use 6x or 600 seconds and 30% less development

The above table represents findings in practical work. The faster films seem to fall into reciprocity effect at shorter exposures, i.e., Royal Pan requires 2x exposure at the 4-second level. The reverse is true of slower film, i.e. Kodak Panatomic-X sheet film requires 4x exposure at 32 seconds or 128 seconds and 40% less development. Each photographer should make tests with various films in the equipment used. The effects of lens-and-camera flare should not be overlooked. And new negative materials are being introduced from time to time — all possessing response characteristics which cannot be anticipated or described here.

4

In the previous section we discussed briefly some of the different types of light sources and their physical properties. We should now consider the methods of measurement of intensity of the principal sources of illumination. The common unit of measurement of light is the footcandle: the intensity of one candle at a distance of one foot. (Refer to PHOTO-LAB-INDEX Section 10 for detailed information on illuminating nomenclature.) There are many other units of specific meaning in technological fields, but since all can be converted to the footcandle, which is simple to understand, we shall limit ourselves to that term here.

Incident-light meters measure illumination in terms of footcandles, with direct conversion to exposure values. A translucent sphere or cone over the meter cell integrates the general illumination; the exposure values are based on the actual intensity of the illumination and the assumed exposure scale and speed of the negative, not the usual reflectivity range of the subject. For average subjects this method will serve to produce good *average* exposure readings in which the principal brightnesses of the subject are represented by values within the exposure scale of the negative. However, such a method does not give information on the *actual* brightnesses of the various areas of the subject, and only implies the total brightness range. This cannot inform us on the actual brightness of any particular area; we therefore cannot visualize the print values of specific areas, and we cannot predefine, before making the exposure, the exposure-development controls so helpful in achieving precise and expressive results. Of course, if we have had a lot of experience with similar subject material, and with incident-light evaluations as well, we can empirically approach a more subtle control. It is my strong personal conviction that the incident-light method is by no means as accurate and flexible as the brightness evaluation method stressed in this book.

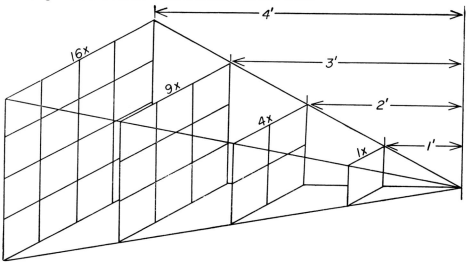

3. Diagram Depicting the Inverse Square Law. The law can be simply stated as: "The intensity of illumination decreases as the square of the distance of the light source increases." A given amount of light covering a given area at 1 foot distance must cover 4 times the area at 2 feet distance, 9 times the area at 3 feet distance.

4. Student Group in Library. Made with Hasselblad Camera, 80mm lens. Interior lighting was balanced with late afternoon daylight on building seen through the window. The problem here was to achieve an illusion of appropriate balance between the interior and exterior values. (See Fig. 35, page 64, for example of too close matching of interior and exterior values.) The basic exposure was determined by the brightness of the building facade (placed on Zone VI) and the sky (which fell on Zone IX). Once this was determined, the next step was to "build" the light on the group to simulate the existing light in the room. Two lights in cone reflectors were directed on the subjects from an angle approximating that of the stand-lamp. The girl's face is illuminated from the light within the lampshade and from the distant light that was directed to the boy on the right. The distant light that was aimed at the boy in the center also gave some illumination to the girl's hair and shoulder and the back of the chair. Ideally, some very careful shielding of the last-mentioned light would have added to the illusion of reality; the only part of the image that does not "convince" the spectator that the picture was made entirely with available light is the extreme left-hand part of the chair and the obvious back-lighting of the girl. The reader should place his thumb over these areas and he will immediately understand this statement. A third light was "bounced" from the wall and ceiling behind the camera to give a slight "boost" to the shadows.

6

A quick résumé of the Zone System will be helpful here: Because of the geometric progression of conventional lens stops (each doubling the exposure values as they progress from small to large—f/32 to f/4, for example), the "gray scale" (the progression of values and tones for maximum black to pure white) can be represented by 10 steps or "zones," as follows:

Zones	Typical Values	Units of Exposure
0	Maximum black; no textural effect	$\frac{1}{2}$
I	First visible step of tone above maximum black	1
II	First impression of texture in shadows	2
III	Satisfactory values of shadow "detail"	4
IV	Average value of shadows in portraits, architecture, etc.	8
V	"Middle gray" (gray card value—18 per cent reflectance)	16
VI	Average Caucasian skin value (36 per cent reflectance)	32
VII	Light gray objects, very light skin	64
VIII	Very light gray—"textured whites"	128
IX	Pure white	256

If we photograph a group of surfaces ranging from 1 to 256 units of brightness, or if we give progressive exposures to a surface of consistent brightness, exposing so that Zone I falls upon the effective threshold of the negative and developing the negative so that Zone VIII exposure will give sufficient density (opacity) to print on a normal paper as a very light gray, we will have demonstrated the relationship of the zones. We will also have determined what "normal" development will be for the particular combination of camera, lens, film, developer and printing process used. Obviously, these conditions vary in practice, and each photographer must determine his own "normal" procedures. (Refer to Book 2, page 39.)

To recapitulate some of the basic terms used in discussion of the Zone System:

1. *Brightness (Luminance) Values:* Relative reflectances of subject.

The reflective values of any surface or substance are modified by the texture and configuration of the surface, the angle and quality of the light, the position of the lens (in relation to the angle of illumination), the color of the subject, and the color response of the film. The contrast (exposure range) of the film must also be considered in relation to the values of the final image.

We measure the brightnesses of surfaces with our exposure meters, and determine not only the brightnesses themselves, but the *range* of the brightnesses of the subject, which we then relate to the exposure scale of the negative. We "visualize" the "placement" of the various brightnesses on the exposure scale of the negative in relation to the desired qualities of the final print.

"Flare" from lens and reflections within the camera can seriously modify the brightness range of the image, raising the shadow values higher than their proportionate values in the subject. The use of coated lenses and of effective lens shades will serve to reduce flare, but the interior of the camera should be thoroughly blackened and baffled to minimize internal reflections.

2. *Negative Density Values:* Relative densities (opacities of the negative). In relation to the Brightness Values, these values are modified by lens and camera flare, and the amount of development given the negative. A low-contrast subject can be "expanded" by increased development, and a high-contrast subject "compacted" by reduced development.

To expand 1 zone, we give "Normal-plus-1 development" — roughly 1.5x normal.

To expand 2 zones, we give "Normal-plus-2 development" — roughly 2x normal.

To compact 1 zone we give "Normal-minus-1 development" — roughly .7x normal.

To compact 2 zones we give "Normal-minus-2 development" — roughly .5x normal.

Two solution development (Book 4, page 78) is advised for control of very high contrast subjects. See table below.

3. *Print Values:* Brilliances (reflective densities of the print image. These should approximate the original visualization of print values.)

Zones (Exposure Zones) relate only to the Exposure scale of the negative (new terminology).

Brightness values can be modified in natural lighting by the use of reflecting screens and/or "fill-in" artificial light. In artificial lighting these values can be adjusted by visual and photometric control of illumination.

The *negative* is planned for a particular printing paper; that which I call a "normal" negative is one that will print in full scale on an average No. 2 projection paper or on an average No. 1 contact paper.

The *print values* are, in a sense, proportionate to the subject brightnesses, although for obvious reasons the values may be intentionally modified. It is clear that a print of maximum brilliancy scale of 1:50 cannot *duplicate* a subject-brightness scale of, say 1:500. (An exception would be with transparencies or lantern slides: here the brilliancy range is much greater, as the values are seen by *transmission of light,* and not by reflection from the print surface.) We visualize in terms of *interpretation,* not literal duplication of values, and our visualization may intentionally be a *departure from reality.*

Data for 2-solution development (Kodak D-23 and 1 per cent Borax or Kodalk solution) as prepared by William Quandt of the Department of Photography, California School of Fine Arts, San Francisco: The film is developed first in the Kodak D-23 solution, then transferred without rinsing to the 1 per cent Kodalk or Borax solution. The indicated times are based on constant agitation of the film in the developer solution, and a few seconds agitation every 30 seconds in the Kodalk or Borax solution. The table below is for Kodak Super-XX sheet film, and for negatives which are to be contact-printed or enlarged with a diffused-light enlarger. Use *fresh* developer, and *always* use fresh Borax or Kodalk solution for each batch of negatives.

DESIRED DEVELOPMENT	TIME IN KODAK D-23, then TIME IN 1% Borax or Kodalk Solution	
Normal	8 minutes	minutes
Normal-minus-1	6 minutes	"
Normal-minus-2	5 minutes	"
Normal-minus-3	4 minutes	"
Normal-minus-4	3 minutes	"
Normal-minus-5	2½ minutes	"
Normal-minus-6	2 minutes	"
Normal-minus-7	1½ minutes	"

The "control" Zone here is Zone VIII; that means that if a brightness value fell on Zone XII, we would apply the "Normal-minus-4" development to achieve a Zone VIII density in the negative. For negatives to be enlarged in condenser-type enlargers, use the next lowest time, i.e. Normal, 6 and 3 minutes; Normal-minus-3, 3 and 3 minutes. Suggestions for other films:

Kodak Tri-X Film: Normal 8 minutes, then 3 minutes in 1 per cent Borax or Kodalk solution.

Adox KB-17 Film: Normal 5½ minutes, then 3 minutes in 1 per cent Borax or Kodalk solution.

New Plus-X Film (Kodak): Normal 7 minutes, then 3 minutes in 1 per cent Borax or Kodalk solution.

Development times for other materials can be worked out by proportionate tests.

Basic Tests for the Polaroid Land Process

With this process the materials have restricted "latitude"; exposures must be rather precise as in color photography. However, it is a relatively simple matter to make tests to confirm effective speeds and to discover the effective exposure ranges of the films.

As the process produces a positive print we can have no doubt as to the accuracy of our computations and exposures, because we can make a direct comparison of the gray card with its Polaroid print image. Because of slight color differences in the gray card and the print we should use a yellow filter (or a Wratten # 90 viewing filter) when making the visual comparisons.

Once we have confirmed the speed of the material in relation to our equipment, we can then proceed to discover the exposure ranges, by making successive exposures of the gray card brightness value on the various zones. We should expose for Zones I, II, III, IV, V, VI, VII, VIII, IX and X. On the basis of matching gray card and Zone V print, we will find that the "useful range" will be about as follows:

Types 42 and 52, with Normal Development, Zones II½ to VII (1 to 24+)

The Polaroid Land Projection Film (Type 46L), has much greater exposure range, and a much higher image contrast than the print material. This quality is very useful in the projection of the transparency images, and an extraordinary brilliancy of image obtains.

Now, the "useful" (or *dynamic* range as Polaroid designates it) indicates the first step above pure black and the first step below pure white, just as with conventional materials. An approximate idea of the "textural ranges" is given below. The term "textural range" is not exact; it relates to the values above black and below white in which "textures" or the impression of "substance" are preserved in the image. This will vary slightly in relation to the subject and the intentions of the photographer. Usually, this range starts one Zone above the lowest "dynamic" Zone, and ends one or one-half zone below the highest "dynamic" zone.

Types 42 and 52, normal development, range Zones III to VI½ (1 to 12+)

More than "normal" development time will add a little density to the lower part of the scale (the deep shadow values of Zones III½, III, II½ and II) without changing the values of Zone VI and higher exposure values. Types 47, 107, and 57 are somewhat "softer" than Types 42 and 52 — that is, they have a longer exposure scale. Type 55 P/N gives a print and a very fine negative. At present the optimum negative speed is a little slower than the optimum print speed, but the manufacturer is working toward equal speed for both. Type 51 is a high-contrast print material (about 1 to 2 exposure range!) for "line" work and other high contrast effects. With the Polaroid MP-3 camera and the Graphic Arts Kit this material has important applications in the offset-reproduction processes. Type 48, 108 and 58 (Polacolor) is discussed in my POLAROID MANUAL (Morgan & Morgan). Detailed descriptions of the various Polaroid Land materials and Polaroid equipment will be found in this book.

9

When the basic Zone V test has been completed, a series of exposures should be made of a white sheet of paper on which thin type or lines are printed. These exposures should encompass Zones I through X, using the brightness of the white paper alone (not the *average* of paper and type) for exposure determination. The images should be fairly large and sharp so that textures (type, delicate lines, etc.) will show. With the lower limit of the dynamic range, the type or lines will be barely visible; with the lower limit of the textural range, they can be clearly seen. Likewise, with the higher limit of the dynamic range, the type or lines will be on the edge of visibility, but at the higher limit of the textural range, they can be "read" against a light gray background.

In conventional photography we follow the "golden rule": "Expose for the shadows and develop for the highlights." But with the Polaroid Land print materials, *we expose for the high values and develop for the shadows.* Assume that 15 seconds at 65° is "normal" developing time for Type 52 film; if, at this time, the whites of the image are good but the blacks weak, increase developing time. If the blacks are good and the whites gray, increase *both* exposure and developing time. A simple rule of thumb is to place the brightest area of the subject on Zone VII and expose accordingly. In this way, "blocking" of important high values will be avoided. As with color photography, exposure is critical; a difference of one-half stop exposure can "gray down" or "block up" an important high brightness area of the subject.

5. Adjusting Microtome Knife (courtesy, University of California). Made with Hasselblad 500C, 80mm Planar, plus Extension tube. Basic illumination was fluorescent ceiling lights, plus bounce light from both walls and ceiling. Direct illumination on knife was from small lamp used for lighting small specimens, etc. This light was adjusted to produce an acute reflection from the side of the knife, Reflection on metal part above was from ceiling lights and could not be controlled with available equipment.

We see all nonluminous objects by their reflected light. Apart from considerations of color, specular (mirror-like), and fluorescent (light-generating) qualities, all nonluminous substances reflect diffuse light in varying degrees in proportion to the amount of illumination (incident light) falling upon them. For example, under sunlight or some consistent source of artificial light, the reflectances of the following substances are approximately as shown:

		Approx. Zones & Rel. Exp. Units	
Black Velvet	2%	II	2
Standard Gray Card	18%	V	16
Average Caucasian Skin..........	36%	VI	32
Light Gray Paper................	70%	VII	64
Magnesium Carbonate	96%	VII-VIII	96

Hence the brightness range of the darkest and lightest substances available is only about 1:48. This is well within the exposure scale of the ordinary negative materials. The combined lens and camera flare of most cameras will serve to further reduce this range to possibly 1:25 or 32 as the *effective* image-brightness range. As the total exposure range of the average negative material is about 1:256 (the modern "useful" range—Zones I to IX inclusive), we can see that we have a considerable "latitude of exposure"; the following placements of 1:32 effective brightness-range are possible:

Zones	I	II	III	IV	V	VI	VII	VIII	IX
Exposure Units.........	1	2	4	8	16	32	64	128	256

```
                      x........................x
                          x........................x
                              x........................x
                                  x........................x
```

Differences of color will modify the relative brightness of these substances, but with panchromatic film and the usually low color saturation of most substances, the color effect is not very significant.

Remember, the demonstration above relates to substances of maximum reflectance-range illuminated by one consistent light source and does not take into consideration shadowed areas. Now let us suppose we are considering the same substances arranged so that they are in both direct consistent illumination *and* consistent shadow illumination; and let us assume the shadow illumination is 1/4 that of the direct illumination (this would assume there was an environment of fairly high reflectance). The range of reflectances would be extended 4 times; that is, the total subject-brightness range would be 1:192. Considering a conservative amount of flare, the image-brightness range might be about 1:100. Obviously our exposure latitude is much less than before.

Zones	I	II	III	IV	V	VI	VII	VIII
Exposure Units..............	1	2	4	8	16	32	64	128

```
                      x................................x
```

Out of doors on a clear day, the ratio of direct sunlight to shadow will be about 8:1. Under such conditions, considering a conservative amount of flare, the image-brightness range might be about 1:256. Now the "latitude" of the negative is at a minimum:

Zones	I	II	III	IV	V	VI	VII	VIII	IX
Exposure Units	1	2	4	8	16	32	64	128	256

x..x

Working with available light indoors (light from fixtures, windows, etc.), we may find much greater brightness-ranges than demonstrated by the last example—but again, our eyes are so marvelously adaptable to wide differences of illumination and brightness that we are not visually aware of the high contrasts under such conditions. We must depend upon accurate measurement.

Let us pause here a moment for a review of the meaning of the "brightness scale." Zone I is but a step above solid black, Zone VIII or IX a step below pure white. Here is where visualization enters: just how do we wish to represent the subject in the final print? Do we want the shadowed black velvet to be Zone I black, or solid black, or Zone II black? This is where the purely mechanical rendition of values breaks down; the camera cannot make decisions for us—cannot supply, by itself, the subtle "departure from reality" which is so important in creative photography. Suppose we have a shadow-to-direct-light range of 1:4; in the table below we will see how the various shadowed and directly lit areas fall on the exposure scale (assuming that the black velvet in shadow will be placed on Zone I):

Subjects	Zones	Exposure Units	Approximate Reflectance
Black velvet in shadow...............	I	1	½ of 1%
	II	2	—
Black velvet in direct light	III	4	2%
Gray card, shadow....................	IV	8	4%
Skin, shadow	V	16	8%
Light gray paper, shadow ⎫ Gray card, direct light ⎬	VI	32	18%
Magnesium, carbonate surface, shadow...	VI-VII	48	24%
Skin, direct light	VII	64	36%
Light gray paper, direct light............	VIII	128	70%
Magnesium carbonate surface, direct light	VIII-IX	192	96%
Bright reflections of light source........	IX and up	256 and up	

Due to the inherent flare of the camera and lens, there would be a lessening of actual image-contrast, but we must remember that we select a "normal" degree of development which will modify this effect when we desire a negative of optimum density (opacity) range. Flare would raise the lower zones perhaps one full zone, but would have no appreciable effect on the higher zones. If we desired our negative to represent density zones from I to VIII-IX, our "normal" development would achieve it. However, we would probably give the above a normal-minus development because we would want to see a *difference* between the diffuse high values of the magnesium carbonate surface and the specular highlight (or actual light source). In other words, the image of the magnesium carbonate should appear as a very slight tone *under* pure white Zone VIII or IX).

The above represents a rather full range of subject-reflectances. The usual subjects have less range. White fabrics and paper reflect up to about 85 per cent, and common dark materials about 4 or 5 per cent; hence the average subject brightness range would be about 1:16 to 1:20. But do not let this confuse you—

12

even with a flare factor of 2x, a direct-light-shadow ratio of 8 would produce an image-brightness range of 1:64 to 1:80.

We are prone to think that just because our negative material has a useful range of 1:128, we can squeeze a 1:128 brightness range within it and achieve a satisfactory image. Remember, if we desire any feeling of substance and texture in our darkest areas, we must place them *no lower* than Zone II (preferably Zone III). We cannot be casual about the lower values; they must be placed adequately to assure the desired effect in the final print, not just arbitrarily placed on Zone I because they happen to be the darkest areas of the subject. In any dark area there may be values representing Zones 0, I, II, and III. If the average of these values is placed below Zone II, it is likely that poor textural rendition will result. If we wish to retain an impression of tone and texture in our lightest areas, we cannot visualize them *higher* than Zone VIII. Of course, while development controls have little effect on the lowest values (Zones I and II), we can exercise considerable control with the high values (as described in Book 2). Nevertheless, the higher the placement of the higher brightnesses, the less textural and tonal effects are retained, no matter how we control the development, because as the exposure increases there is an increased scatter of light *within* the emulsion, and fine details may be obscured. The result is observed as a "blocked" white or light gray. ("Tanning" or "surface" developers, such as Pyro and Pyrocatechin, give better textured whites than do developers containing much sodium sulfite, such as D-23, D-76, etc., which tend to dissolve and diffuse silver throughout the emulsion, especially in areas of high density.)

Brightness Measurement

This is an extremely important subject and one that relates to the foundations of careful thinking and planning about photography. If we accept the fact that we are making photographs with the light reflected from the subject, it will then be obvious that an accurate evaluation of this reflected light is vital to positive results. The infinite variations of subject-contrast, the complex reflection and environmental effects (to which the eye readily adapts itself), combine to produce difficult problems in the evaluation of subject brightnesses. This is especially true with artificial-light photography as opposed to natural-light photography (which is not affected by the Inverse Square Law effect). Hence the proper use of an adequate exposure meter is essential to satisfactory work with artificial light. The value of a meter such as the S.E.I. Exposure Photometer (which permits readings of very small areas of the subject with a very high degree of accuracy) will be obvious to those who demand precise control of subject-brightnesses and exposures.

My opinion of the Weston Master Meter (and other meters of the same order of sensitivity) is of the highest, and I use the Weston for a considerable part of my work. The Weston Master V meter incorporates the EV numbers as well as its own exposure value numbers (of which #12=100 c/ft^2, and the other numbers are geometrically related — #13=200 c/ft^2 and #11=50 c/ft^2, etc.). The new Weston Ranger IX meter has an extended sensitivity range, a new Exposure-Value number system (in which #10=1 c/ft^2 and #16=64 c/ft^2, etc.) and an optional Zone System calculating dial. It has a much narrower field of view (about 18°) in comparison with the 30° field of view of other Weston meters. The use of extension tubes before the cell reduces the field of view to any desired degree, but with them, less light is transmitted to the photocell and the minimum sensitivity of the meter is further reduced. (Not advised for the Ranger IX.)

My recommendation in favor of highly sensitive and accurate meters (such as the S.E.I. Photometer, made by the Salford Electrical Industries, England, and the new Spectra Brightness Spot Meter, made by the Photo-Research Corporation, Burbank, California) sometimes meets with criticism on the basis of high cost. In serious photography such meters will soon pay for themselves in time and materials saved, and in the satisfaction of achieving positive results. The casual snapshooter has no real need for such instruments of precision, but the serious amateur and professional photographer will benefit tremendously from their use.

Whatever measuring devices we use, three principal methods are available.
1. The incident-light method.
2. The reflection-brightness method.
3. The gray-card interpolation method.

We have discussed the first two methods and will concentrate largely on the second method throughout this book (the direct measurement of subject-reflectivities). However, the third method has certain advantages and can be described thus:

The standard gray card has a reflectance of about 18 per cent, which logically belongs on Zone V of the exposure scale. Obviously, as will be seen in the table below, a wide range of reflectances will be placed on the scale if this gray card value is placed on Zone V (Highest reflectance 96% falls between VII and VIII):

Zones	I	II	III	IV	V	VI	VII	x	VIII
% Brightness	(1.13)	2.25	4.5	9	18	36	72	(96)	
(Approx. relative Values) ..	1	2	4	8	16	32	64	96	(128)

Hence if the brightness range of the subject does not exceed the above, the negative will represent all values within its scale of densities. Of course, as mentioned before, this does not give us any idea of the specific brightnesses—it only tells us what brightnesses will be included in the scale. It does not give us the opportunity to specifically "place" the lower values as desired on the exposure scale, or to exercise the control of high-value densities by development procedures. The scale above represents only the reflectances of the subject under a single consistent lighting, and without shadow values. Under normal conditions, if a reading of the gray card gave, say, 25 c/ft², the interpolated brightnesses for the other Zones would be: (assuming, of course, "light-and-shade" illumination):

Zones	I	II	III	IV	V	VI	VII	VIII
C/ft²	1.6	3.2	6.5	13	25	50	100	200

As we have seen in Book 2, page 28, the brightness value in c/ft² opposite Zone V is the reciprocal of the exposure in fractions of a second; with a film of speed ASA 64, it would be 1/25 second at f/8; with a film speed of ASA 125, it would be 1/25 second at f/11. Tungsten light speeds are figured in proportion; a tungsten speed of ASA 40 would indicate 1/25 second at between f/5.6 and f/8 (about ⅔ stop above f/5.6, etc.)

If our meter will not permit us to measure all values of the subject because of insufficient sensitivity, we can make the directly illuminated brightness readings as well as a gray card reading, under direct light. We can, then, evaluate the shadowed values by taking the reading of the gray card in the shadowed position. If it reads ¼ or ⅛ the value in direct light, we know that the brightness of *the same subject surfaces* in shadow will be ¼ or ⅛ the brightnesses in direct light. Their *effective* brightnesses in the image may be raised by flare.

6. Dr. W. Albert Noyes and Chemical Equipment. The first problem here was to illuminate the head and hand of the chemist advantageously, and avoid confusion with the complicated equipment. For reproduction, the relatively small head demanded a certain "brilliancy" and isolation. One light in a cone reflector provided the main illuminaton, and the shadow side of the face was illuminated from a white card. There was a small "axis" light at the lens to provide more light on the face and produce catchlights in the eyes. Several lights placed rather high created "glitter" in the complex glass and metal assembly. The background was intentionally left unlighted, so as not to confuse the intricate patterns of the subject. A 4x5 view camera and a 5-inch lens were used. The slight convergence is intentional.

A light source burning in space projects an equal value of illumination in all directions, and this illumination is strictly dominated by the Inverse Square Law (at twice the distance the illumination is 1/4 the power. See Fig. 3). When burning against a flat diffuse reflecting surface, its illuminating power is considerably increased in a directional sense and is, of course, greatest along a line perpendicular to the surface of the reflector. (See Fig. 7a.) The Inverse Square Law holds all angles to this flat reflecting surface. But when the light is burning in a curved reflector, the greater part of the light—in fact, practically all of it—is directed in a somewhat narrow cone of illumination, and the illuminating power is increased to a marked degree. (See Fig. 7b.)

It is my opinion that it would be easier to make practical tests with all of the reflectors used and set down their respective light-producing values at various distances in the basic notebook, rather than have to calculate the effective intensity of the lights every time they were used. For steady-burning lamps, direct brightness readings are advised, but exposure tests will be necessary with flashlamps.

Spotlights have definite optical qualities which will be discussed later. The quality of the reflecting surface also affects the quality of the light; a soft diffusing surface gives a relatively soft, evenly distributed illumination; a highly polished surface will yield a sharp, and sometimes uneven illumination.

We are accustomed to the normal "edge quality" of shadows produced by sunlight. This "edge" depends upon the angle subtended by the disk of the sun—about 1/2 degree. If we illuminate a subject with a light source whose illuminating area subtends 1/2 a degree, we will get approximately the same effect as with sunlight. As this angle becomes broader, we will have both softer and broader shadows and highlights. Everyone is aware of the very broad highlights on portraits when the diffuse reflector is placed too close to the subject. In sunlight, of course, there are two modifying factors: the brilliancy of the sun is not limited only to its disk, but to the adjacent area of intense atmospheric flare; and the skylight is generally diffuse. The quality of skylight is difficult to reproduce indoors. Much diffused light used in studio photography comes from the side, while the predominant amount of skylight is largely from above and is "enveloping." We should not feel it imperative to *reproduce* daylight and sunlight, for artificial light gives great opportunity for modulation of form and tonal contrasts.

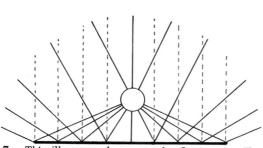 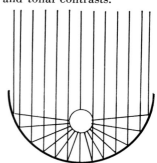

7a. This illustrates the scattered reflections from a flat surface. A polished surface will reflect more light than a "soft" diffusing surface, and will have a "sharper" quality.

7b. This illustrates the "directional" reflections from a curved reflector, concentrating the light in a relatively narrow angle. The shape of the curve modifies the angle of light

Subjects Viewed from Camera Position

It is of real importance that the subject be studied and evaluated from the camera position. Not only are compositional effects altered by a slight change in viewpoint, but lighting effects may vary in relation to the viewing angle. Sometimes only a change of a few inches in viewpoint will obscure an important highlight, or a vital shadow edge. The closer the lights to the subject, the more such differences will be noticed. This is especially true when photographing flat objects such as paintings; a distracting glare at one corner might not be observed by the eye at a foot to the right or left of the lens. The single-lens reflex cameras (Graflex, Hasselblad, etc.) are ideal in that the photographer sees exactly what the lens sees.

It should be mentioned here that the usual cut corners of ground-glass focusing screens sometimes hide distressing details in the image corners; have your ground glass fill the *entire* area of the focusing screen! A round hole can be made in the center of the ground glass; this provides for escape of air when the bellows are closed and also makes possible critical focusing on the aerial image.

8. Oscilloscope. The main light was on the man on the left, and this light was picked up by the man above the oscilloscope. Another light was directed to the background wall. Environmental light only on the oscilloscope itself—to permit "signal" to show.

17

9. Vronsky and Babin, Duo-Pianists. This was a difficult subject to compose; the "nested" position of the two grand pianos created a considerable depth-of-field problem, requiring use of a long lens (14-inch) on a 4x5 camera placed about 25 feet from the foreground figure. The camera might have been placed nearer the foreground figure (and the depth-of-field controlled by use of a smaller lens stop on a relatively short-focus lens), but emphasis of scale would then fall upon the foreground figure and the idea of artistic "equality" of both members of the team would not have been achieved. It was important to separate the figures decisively from the background—the man against the light background and the woman's profile against the dark interior of the piano. Flashlamps were used as follows: One light to right for woman's profile; one light above the man's head; one light "bounced" from white screen on left (to support shadows), and one light against light background. "Finding" or modeling lights were employed to compose, and relative brightnesses were measured with the S.E.I. Meter. The actual exposure was adjusted to give Zone VI value to the woman's arm (the highlights on arm and head approach Zone VII).

18

AN APPROACH TO LIGHTING

As with many aspects of photography, the problem of artificial lighting is usually attacked in reverse! The student often starts with lighting formulas without a clear realization of the structural and expressive effects of controlled lighting in relation to his subject or his concept. Perhaps no formulas or "methods" in photography are as dangerous to creative achievement as are the conventional "rules" of lighting! Rules, after all, are but the integration of successful organization; the most creative people produce their own expressive formulas.

Rather than begin the study of artificial lighting *with* light, we will begin *without* light, thinking in shape and volume in a tactile, spacial sense. We will work first with the simple form of a cube. The cube should be 6 to 12 inches in diameter, of smooth material and painted dead matte white. In a darkened room, or with the eyes closed, the cube must be handled until a physical appraisal of its shape and volume, surface and edge, is grasped. We arrive first at an awareness of this object by non-visual means.

Our first visual and photographic experience with the cube is that of a silhouette—wherein only the outline of its form appears against a light background (Fig. 10a). Combining our tactile appreciation of this object with the visual, the outline will confirm solidity, thereby indicating how involved is our instinctive comprehension of the external world. One part of our mind *knows* that the cube is a volume; another *sees* it as an outline—but it is *recognized* as a cube!

The next step is to see and photograph the cube in a completely flat "axis" light—that is, light from a point close to the axis of the lens and preferably directed from behind the focal plane of the camera. The axis light, in order to achieve its purpose—that is, to fill every part of the subject as seen from the lens with a consistent value of illumination—should be behind the camera; if it is in front of the

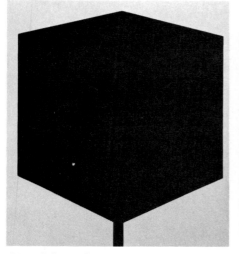 

10a. Cube in Silhouette. A powerful light was thrown on the background, and the cube itself shielded from environmental light. The area where the cube was photographed was enclosed with black drapes.

10b. Cube in Flat Light. This picture was made with a diffused light behind the camera. Because of a small amount of environmental light in the room, the cube form can be vaguely seen.

camera, the shadows cast by the subject would appear in the background *larger* than the object itself. The ideal light for this purpose would be a ring tube encircling the camera at the focal plane. If the three visible faces of the cube are all at approximately the same angle to the lens axis (and to the light), all will have approximately the same brightness value (Fig. 10b). Our background here should be quite light or quite dark.

Next, while retaining the axis light (although with reduced intensity) we add a light from the side, illuminating the top and one side of the cube. If the top and side surfaces are at the same angle to the sidelight, both values will be approximately the same; if the angles differ, one or the other will be brighter (as seen from the lens). With this setup, we have a composition of 3 brightness values: the background, the cube side under axis light, and the cube side (and/or top) under the sidelight. (Figs. 11a and b; Fig. 12a.) *Caution:* In testing, be certain the lights are sufficiently distant from the cube to overcome the inverse square effect; with a cube 12 inches across, the lights should be about 8 feet distant to assure adequately consistent illumination.

Now add another light on the side opposite the first sidelight, or increase the intensity of the axis light, and/or increase or decrease the value of the background light, thereby achieving a wide range of differences of illumination on the cube and its environment. Or eliminate the axis (or second light) entirely and obtain an image of harsh contrast (Fig. 12b.). Of course, environmental reflections will modify the values of the surfaces which are weakly lighted; hence the importance of making this simple test out of doors or in a very dark-walled room where such reflections are usually inconsequential.

In addition, we may add a top or "decorative" light, which will increase the brightness of the upper surface of the cube; we then have a clear-cut composition of 4 values: one side, axis only; one side, sidelight (plus axis light); one side,

11a. Here the cube has been photographed under two lights (with a glancing illumination of the top from the sidelight). The background is on Zone I. Other Zones represented are: IV, V, and VII.

11b. Here the cube has been photographed under the same disposition of lighting as in 11a, except that brightnesses (in relation to background) have been raised to Zones V, VI and VIII.

20

decorative light (plus axis light and sidelight); and background. (Fig. 13a.)

This is elementary, except for important "creative" questions—*how* bright should the 4 surfaces be? Can their brightnesses be controlled, and in what terms? Is it possible to achieve a definitely *planned* organization of brightnesses?

Interpretation of the cube in terms of brightnesses is limited only by our imagination and the limitations of the photographic processes. In the sequence of images (Figs. 11 to 13), we see some of the various possibilities of compositional control; numerous others are feasible. In each case we have "placed" the brightnesses on various Zones of the exposure scale; no separation of value is less than one Zone. How is this separation obtained? By careful evaluation of the brightness of each surface of the cube, and of the background, with an appropriate exposure meter. If the cube is large, say about 12 inches across, and if the light is sufficiently intense, the standard Weston Meter can be used with good results. But if it is small, the S.E.I. meter is advised for accurate results—especially if the brightnesses are of relatively low value.

Let us suppose we desire the background to fall on Zone I and the 3 surfaces of the cube on Zones III, V and VII, respectively. If we consider the exposure value of Zone I as one unit of exposure, then Zones III, V and VII will require 4, 16 and 64 units of exposure (see pages 7 and 12, and also Books 2 and 4). As all values will be exposed at once, it must be obvious that the brightnesses should be brought to a 1, 4, 16 and 64 ratio. The brightnesses may be achieved by controlling the intensity of the lights, or changing the distance of the lights from the subject. At any event, the intensities of the lights are adjusted so that the brightnesses of the subject appear as desired, and are confirmed by exposure-meter readings.

12a. Here the cube has been photographed with almost the same plane of lighting as in 11a and 11b, but the brightnesses are now on Zones VII, VIII and IX. The higher Zones are visually compacted. Reproductions of this type cannot hold all the subtleties of values possessed by the original pictures, but broad differences of tone are conveyed here.

12b. Here the cube has been photographed against a background of Zone III value. A strong light on the right gives that side of the cube Zone IX value. The left side of the cube is on Zone I and the top is of Zone II value. The top of the cube was raised a little by environmental light from a rather light ceiling.

13a. Sidelighting of cube about the same as in Figures 11a and 11b, but "top" light applied from spotlight, which gives a Zone IX value. As Zone IX represents pure white in the print, any "glare" or direct reflections would not be seen above the general high level of tone, but would appear above a general Zone VIII value. Hence, if glare is desired, place "ground" value on VIII.

13b. This represents a variable background —the values of the right-hand part of the background approach those of the left-hand side of the cube, and vice versa. This suggests a means of achieving tonal contrast without exaggerating the values of the subject itself. The rather light top of the cube is almost too close in value to the left side background and weakness of form results.

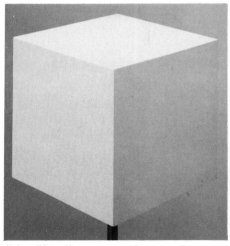

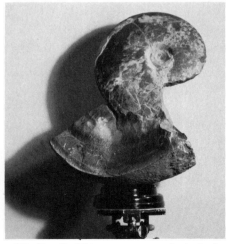

14a. This illustrates an almost total merger of subject and background value (right side of cube and background). Frequently, merging areas may have the same *brightness*, but different *color*, and the eye enjoys a distinction between them which black-and-white photography may fail to capture. Viewing the subject through a Wratten No. 90 Filter will usually reveal such mergers of values.

15. Fossil. This represents a bad shadow which disturbs the formal clarity of the subject. It is a common defect of many pictures made in artificial light; the eye "follows" the line and form of the subject and perceives color differences, but unless accurate visualization is practiced, bad "mergers" such as this will occur. Shadows may be *useful*, but they should not obscure form.

22

Visually, intellectually and emotionally, the eye and mind often perceive the subject in "space," and we are aware of background deficiencies *after* the negative is developed! Relating background and subject demands careful planning and observation. It is important that the picture can be composed *from the position of the lens;* here is where the single-lens reflex cameras function so well, and of course view cameras give us the exact image on the ground glass.

Tonally, we can assume that brightness values of subject and background should be separated by *at least* one Zone; this is especially true in pictures made for reproduction. Color differences between subject and background may be misleading in black-and-white photography; a viewing filter (Wratten No. 90) used visually, or on the lens while composing, is very helpful. If we compose with the lens at full aperture and then stop down, we may find that background details, not observed with the lens wide open, come into sharp focus and distract the forms, edges and textures of the subject, as well as create troublesome mergers of value.

16. Street Scene. A synchro-sunlight picture which attempts to capture the impression of light and shadow on a hot afternoon. One flashlamp was placed several feet to the left of the camera. It would have been better to use a "bounce" light (thereby minimizing secondary shadows in the coat of the woman to the left), but working conditions did not permit. The flashlamp was in a 12-inch reflector, which gave a softer shadow-line than the usual press-type flash reflector; but it did not acheive a sufficiently diffuse illumination. The relative values of the shaded figures under the awning and the sunny areas beyond are in good balance; that is, they suggest a "reality" of visual experience. Pictures such as this, completely unposed and "candid," do not allow much opportunity for detailed planning; the general conditions are observed, the lighting ratio established, and the photographer awaits the most effective moment. A Zeiss Juwel 3¼x4¼ camera was used, with a 4-inch Zeiss-Goerz wide-angle lens. Normal water-bath development was given the negative to avoid "blocking" of the brilliant sunlit areas of the sidewalk and to support the shadows. The exposure was 1/100 second—sufficient to arrest movement of the pedestrians.

The "limb" effect, discussed in Book 4, page 8, is simply achieved with a controlled artificial light; axis light is used for maximum effect. See Figure 17 a and b, wherein the edge of the sphere (the "limb") appears as a dark ring against a light background, and as a dark and vaguely blending area against a dark background. In both instances only the brightness of the background has been changed.

Speaking again of shadows falling upon background—and with especial emphasis on shadows from axis illumination—it will be apparent that if the light is placed in front of the lens plane, the shadow will be larger than the subject; if placed behind the lens plane, the shadow will be smaller and therefore will not be seen in the image. Up or down, right or left positions of the light in reference to the lens axis will place the shadow in counter-position to the direction of the light on the subject. A broad source of light at the camera will cast a partial shadow (a penumbra) around the image of the subject. Here again, considerable experimentation in this field is advised so that the photographer will become aware of the often distressing vagaries of shadow effects. It is suggested that several experiments be made with definite "planned" brightness compositions, giving "normal" development to the negative. (See Book 2, page 40.)

The Polaroid Land Process is ideal for tests such as presented here. We should remember, however, that the scale of values is more or less rigid in the Polaroid Land Process; in conventional photography we have longer exposure scales and exposure-development controls (refer to pages 9 and 10).

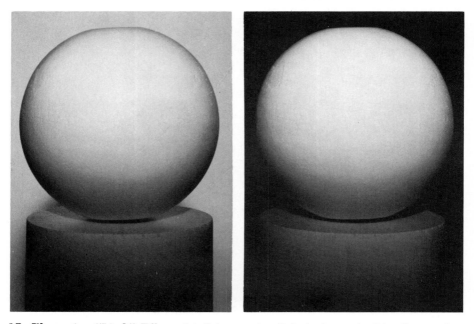

17. Illustrating "Limb" Effect. (a) Sphere against light background; (b) sphere against dark background. The exposures and the lighting on the sphere were identical. Note that the white background is reflected onto the top of the cylinder in (a). The light was on axis, but slightly above the lens; this position produced a small shadow under the sphere. Note that the sphere appears larger in (a); in (b) the shadow area is absorbed into the background.

The simple example of the cube relates to a white object; no color problem was introduced. With colored surfaces or surfaces of low reflectivity, visualization is more difficult; but, as with subjects under natural light, a Wratten Viewing Filter (No. 90) will be found helpful; colored objects viewed through this filter appear somewhat in monochrome, and the relative brightnesses of the colored surfaces are better appreciated.

Here we should discuss a matter which is generally confusing to the non-technical photographer. We know that the eye, the sensitive film and the photo-electric exposure meter do not possess the same sensitivity to different colors of light. A red surface measuring 10 c/ft^2 will not produce the same density in the negative as a green surface of the same *measured* brightness. However, this fact applies mostly to intense, high-saturated colored surfaces. Normally the color saturation of most subjects before the camera is quite low, and the color sensitivity problem becomes quite inconsequential. When working with panchromatic film and intense color, some compensation may be necessary, especially for the blues and reds. The meter, eye and orthochromatic film have about the same sensitivity to green light, but panchromatic film has a lower response to green; therefore some compensation is necessary—the brightness values of strong green objects should be placed about one Zone *higher* on the exposure scale than normally visualized, when using panchromatic film.

18. Hanging Hides (courtesy A. K. Salz Co.). This represents a problem of accentuating subjects of monotonous tone by strong sidelighting. Two lights were used—one from the left on the figure, angled so as to avoid his shadow on the leather, and the other from the far right to "edge-light" the hanging leather. No fill-in light was used; the shadows on the leather were illuminated by reflectance from the brilliantly lit areas of the hides.

25

Shadows on a simple background are troublesome enough, but shadows falling upon important parts of the subject are even more distressing. This brings us to an important aspect of visualization: careful scanning of the subject for defects of lighting, merging of values, unpleasant shadows, distracting highlights and other faults which might not always be apparent to the casual eye. We seldom realize how casual and incomplete our viewing of the external world may be. The mind can construct an entire world on the evidence of a hasty glance; likewise, disturbing details of reality can be completely overlooked but shockingly revealed in the final print! Every area, especially every edge, should be scanned and studied with care. Twin-lens cameras, and cameras with finders above or to one side of the lens, present parallax problems when working with near objects. The parallax can be adjusted to a single plane, but the relationship of this plane to the planes beyond is not indicated, and distracting mergers, etc., may appear unexpectedly in the photograph. We can overcome this unfortunate effect by moving the camera lens into the position occupied by the finding lens. However, this is almost impossible to do when working rapidly with the camera held in the hand. View cameras and single-lens reflex cameras are free of this defect.

In natural light under the sky there is a broad and general level of illumination, and we seldom find black pockets of deep shadow (except under trees, etc.); but with artificial light the potential contrast of the image is severe, and any area of the subject which is shielded from the principal light sources may appear dark and empty. This depends upon environmental reflections, of course. In a small, light-walled room, for example, it would be difficult to achieve a completely "empty" area of tone.

It is of the utmost importance to recognize that the eye can "see" into areas of very low brightness, and encompass a range of brightness far beyond the capacity of the photographic film to record. Hence the necessity of visualizing the final print; first to visualize the rendition of the darkest shadow areas (which will determine the exposure); then to visualize the rendition of the high values (which will determine the amount of illumination used and/or the amount and character of the development given the negative).

In addition, very low levels of illumination demanding long exposures may cause a reciprocity effect, further depreciating the effective brightnesses of the subject and increasing its photographic contrast. (See page 4.) "Smoothness" of tonal values should be sought in all normal work; this can be approached by using the following forms of illumination:

1. "Environmental" light from light walls, screens, etc., suggesting the diffuse qualities of skylight;
2. Directed diffuse light from reflecting screens; and
3. Axis light (fill-in light without apparent shadow effects).

We must not overlook the Inverse Square Law when using the axis light; objects nearest the lens will receive the most light, and distant objects progressively less light. This effect may or may not be desirable; the brightnesses should be checked and visualized with care.

What should the intensity of the fill-in light be? In our demonstrations with the cube, we assumed that the reflectances of the cube surfaces and the background were all the same. However, we will find that most subjects present a wide range of reflectances (as well as variations of color), and the intensity of fill-in light would then depend upon such variations of subject brightnesses. For precise control, brightness values should be carefully measured in all important parts of the subject. This is not difficult when the subject is illuminated by steady-burning lamps; with flash it is far more complex. (See page 34.)

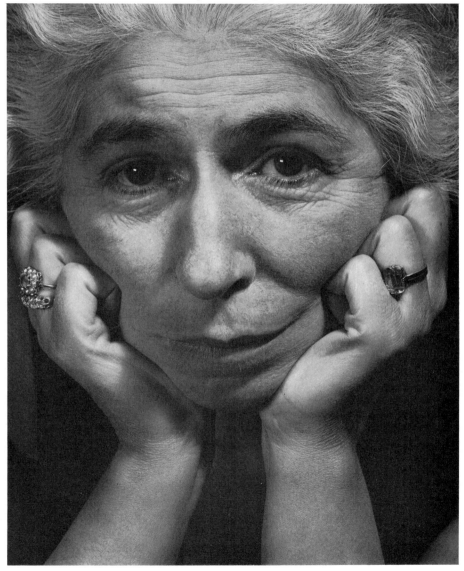

19. Phyllis Bottome, Author. Made with two flashlamps, each in a rectangular light-box (note shape of catchlights in the eyes). One light 6 feet from subject, the other light 12 feet distant (1:4 illumination ratio). A direct, unretouched portrait made on 4x5 negative.

When working with natural light we read the brightness values of the various parts of the subject, placing them on the exposure scale where desired, but always in proper relationship to their mathematical values. We think of these values in terms of Exposure Units—Zone I representing 1 unit, and the other zones representing 2, 4, 8, 16, 32, 64, 128 and 256 units (see page 7). We can add additional light (by reflecting screens or flashlamps) in terms of exposure units, to subjects under natural light (see Book 4, page 94, and page 23 herein). For example, confronted with a subject of high contrast, such as a figure partially in sunlight in a forest environment, where the shadows were of very low brightness value, we would place the sunlit areas on their proper Zones and "boost" the shadowed areas to a level required by our visualization of the final print. Let us assume that the brightness of the sunlit skin (400 c/ft²) represents a desired Zone VII value and is placed on Zone VII of the exposure scale (in this case, one Zone higher than "normal" skin value). If we find that the skin value in shadow is 13 c/ft², it must fall on Zone II, representing 2 units of exposure. Exposing according to this placement would give us a harsh, bleak image which in no way would represent the desired mood of the quiet enveloping light of the forest scene. If we have visualized the skin-in-shadow as a Zone V value, we must either place this value (13 c/ft²) on Zone V, representing 16 units of exposure—thereby grossly overexposing the sunlit areas—or add about 14 units of exposure to this shadowed area. If we use reflecting screens or steady-burning lamps for this purpose, we can measure the values directly, increasing the illumination until it approximates 100 c/ft² on the skin-in-shadow areas. If we use flash, we will be obliged to refer to our Guide Number tables (see page 36) to determine the proper lamp and lamp-to-subject distance for obtaining the desired quantity of light. Our object is to provide a total of 16 units of exposure for the skin surface in shadow; (to repeat, this area already possesses 2 units in existing light, and we must add 14 units more to achieve Zone V brightness value). Hence we speak of *Exposure Units* when thinking of *brightness*—we expose our film to light values *reflected from the subject.*

When we add illumination to the subject in any amount, the brightnesses increase in proportion to the reflectances. In this case of skin in sun and in shadow, while we had extremes of illumination resulting in Zones II and VII brightnesses for the same substance, we added sufficient light to raise the skin in shadow to about Zone V value (remember—the *reflectance* of the skin is practically the same in sun or shade, but its *brightness* depends upon the intensity of the light falling upon it). Another substance—say a tree trunk—which had a brightness of 100 c/ft² in sun (and fell on Zone V) would, in shadow, fall on Zone 0, and with the addition of 14 units of illumination be raised to about Zone IV brightness. In round figures, we could add 16 units; the difference between 14 and 16 units would be too slight to matter seriously. Keep values in geometric sequence whenever feasible—2, 4, 8, 16, 32, etc., as this sequence relates to lens-stop progression.

We have arbitrarily considered one exposure unit as that amount of reflected light which would produce a Zone I density in the negative (0.1 density above film-base-fog density). Two units is represented by Zone II; 4 units by Zone III, and so on in geometric progression; 16 units gives a Zone V value (approximately "gray-card" value), and 32 units gives a Zone VI value (approximately average skin value). Now, if we illuminate a gray card (or any card of any reflecting value) and place its brightness on Zone I of the scale, we will get a Zone I exposure; if we increase the exposure 32 times, we get a Zone VI exposure. If we have a surface of 2 per cent reflectance and one of 64 per cent reflectance, and expose them together so that the 2 per cent surface is rendered as a Zone I value, the 64 per cent surface will appear as a Zone VI value. If the 2 per cent value is rendered as a Zone II value, the 64 per cent surface will appear on Zone VII. Reflectances remain constant, but both illumination and exposure time may be changed to achieve the desired image values. The reader should grasp thoroughly this important basic fact of photography and demonstrate it to himself by actual experiments in the field.

We have "keyed" the Exposure-unit scale to the Zone scale with 32 units opposite Zone VI; if average skin value (about 36 per cent reflectance) is placed on Zone VI, Zone VI exposure value results. If we give skin 16 units, it falls on Zone V; 8 units and it falls on Zone IV, and so on. All related zones of brightness move along proportionately. So when we say we will apply 16 units of exposure, we are giving 1/2 normal exposure; when we apply 8 exposure units, we are giving 1/4 normal exposure, etc., in relation to skin values on Zone VI.

Accumulated exposure units affect the lower zones of the scale, but have increasingly little effect towards the top of the scale. For example, if we add sufficient light to raise a Zone II value to Zone V (14 units added), the Zone VII value (64 units) is raised to 78 units (about 1/4 stop). However, the same amount of light added to Zone VI would increase the 32 units to 46 units (almost 1/2 stop). The very sad results of many synchro-sunlight pictures—the severe "blocking up" of skin values, for example—come from adding 32 units or more to an existing 32 units, thereby doubling the exposure value and flattening out the subtle tonal passages of the subject. We should recognize that the power of flash-lamps is augmented by reflecting walls; synchro-sunlight values are based on the power of flashlamps and reflectors in a nonreflecting environment. As on page 36, tests should be made in such an environment to establish basic illumination values.

We may use the term *Illumination Units* when we speak of the intensity of incident light falling on the subject. For example, illuminate a gray card with an amount of light sufficient to produce a brightness reading of 1.6 c/ft². Place this value on Zone I of the exposure scale and, in a relative sense, consider the incident-light value on the card as representing one unit of illumination. By doubling the intensity of the incident light falling on the card, we effectively raise the placement to Zone II and can consider the incident-light value as representing 2 units of illumination. If we again double the intensity of the incident light on the card, we achieve a Zone III placement and can consider the incident-light value as representing 4 units of illumination. And so on up the scale (64 illumination units on the card would represent a Zone VII placement). Hence:

Exposure Units relate to subject-brightness values.
Illumination Units relate to incident-light values.

Both units, in relation to exposure zones, progress geometrically on the exposure scale. The terms are interchangeable, except that *illumination units will not indicate actual exposure values unless the reflectance of the subject is known.*

29

For many photographers this will be their first experience with "planned" brightness compositions and controlled lighting; the casual evaluations of the eye are often unsatisfactory for precise requirements.

Later we shall see how this approach is applied to expressive photography. It is not a difficult concept; it is only a form of visualization (see Book 4, page 36). This approach is not made with the invidious desire to create new and different problems and methods; it represents a fundamental approach to the logic of photographic art. Perhaps the most perplexing element of this logic lies in its simplicity! In the vast majority of cases the beginner will first apply the "main" light and then add light more or less fortuitously until the subject before him *seems* properly lighted. The two basic faults with this procedure are: (1) his visualization may not be adequate to begin with (visualization of the final print, not of the aspect of the subject alone), and (2) his "eye" is incapable of properly evaluating the related brightnesses of the subject. An exception to the latter statement would exist when the photographer has had considerable experience with *similar subjects* under *similar conditions*. He may "hit it off" with many of his assignments. But there is always a large gap between what is "acceptable" and what is "exceptional." Nothing grants us such freedom of expression as a completely controlled technique.

Hence, this chapter has considerable significance in relation to the approach to photography as presented in this series of books. It reiterates the need for visualization of the final print. Under controlled light this visualization can be more fluent and varied than under natural light.

It shows how the Zone divisions of the gray scale are important pivots of tonal visualization, and by direct inference, how the Zone system of visualization, and exposure and development of the negative, can assure positive results.

The preceding BASIC PHOTO books should be reviewed for clarification of the general approach. In the PHOTO-LAB-INDEX (by John S. Carroll—Morgan & Morgan, Inc., New York) will be found copious data on illumination and allied subjects in far more detailed listing than can be presented in these books.

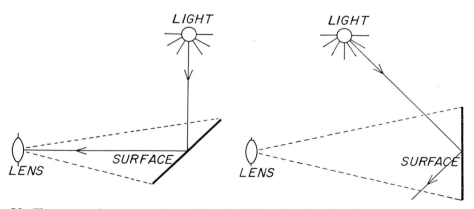

20. The gray card, or any testing surface, should be placed so that, from the lens position, maximum diffuse reflection and minimum glare are achieved, as shown at right.

21. Electric Typewriter Assembly. Made with Hasselblad Super-wide camera. Exisiting light from fluorescent ceiling lights, plus one tungsten light directly above center of subject, to produce some highlights on metal and on the forehead of the technician. This type of soft lighting usually requires less than normal exposure and increased development. (With small negatives, increased development may produce coarser grain; hence normal development and use of a more contrasty paper is suggested.) Two-solution development supports shadows.

22. Dr. C. W. de Kiewiet, President of the University of Rochester. Made with Hassel-blad Camera with 135mm Ektar lens. This picture was planned for reproduction in a well-printed brochure. The values are too close for newspaper reproduction (which requires—for the most brilliant results—black, white, and not more than 3 steps of tone between. This portrait was made with one main light on the right, one top light, and one light "bounced" from a white surface behind the camera, plus a small catchlight lamp near the lens. The glasses were appar-ently coated lenses, as reflections are at a minimum.

EVALUATION OF EQUIPMENT

It is extremely important that the photographer thoroughly understand his equipment. It is assumed that he has checked his camera and lenses (see Book 1, pages 113-115), and that he has established exposure-development standards for his lenses, cameras, film and developers used in relation to his desired image qualities. (See Book 2, and page 7 herein.)

When he approaches photography by artificial light, he must add important lighting items to his equipment, and these must be carefully checked and evaluated. He must *know* the effective illuminating values of his lamps, reflectors, reflecting screens, and other pieces of equipment. He must *know* the proper guide numbers for his flash equipment, and the proper guide numbers and developing times for negatives made with speedlamps. This section will be devoted to description of essential tests which every photographer should make with his own equipment. The object is for him to obtain the images he personally desires as expressive of his personal concepts—not merely to obtain a "standard" negative. Manufacturers' recommendations are adequate as *points of departure*, and they are invaluable for comparative purposes when the photographer has established his own values.

Needless to say, all electrical equipment must be shockproof (of vital importance with speedlamps), of fine quality and dependability, and of efficient construction and design. Reduce equipment to an effective minimum and avoid unnecessary gadgets and odds and ends. Keep reflectors polished and clean, and use fresh batteries only. Check all contacts in plugs, sockets, connections, etc. Test all equipment frequently, including synchronizing shutters and their connections. When using powerful tungsten lamps and photofloods, watch for possible heat damage and fire hazards. *Carry extra fuses*—both standard 15-20 amp. line fuses and special fuses for equipment. Also carry spare floodlamps and ample numbers of flashlamps. Test speedlight batteries *frequently* and keep connections clean. A check list is advisable, even for the most orderly photographer!

Tungsten and Photoflood Lamps

With continuous light sources, the effective illumination can be evaluated with an exposure meter. Testing for these light sources is therefore chiefly directed to exposure-development determinations. The reflectors used, however, should be checked for efficient distribution of light, and the efficiency of different reflectors (in terms of total output) carefully checked and recorded for reference. As it is probable that the reflectors will be used for both flood and flashlamps, it is advisable to test them for relative output as the first step in the testing plan.

With a given lamp, reflector B might put out 1.5x as much light as reflector A. Reflector C might have 3/4 the output of A at the same distance from the subject because of its diameter and diffusion characteristics.

Using the Kodak Neutral Test Card for these tests, comparative efficiency is determined by placing the reflectors at a given distance from the test surface, using the same lamp for all tests, keeping the surface of the card at about 45° to the direction of the light, and directing the exposure meter at the same angle to the card for all readings. Meters such as the Weston should be read at the same distance from the card in every case so that the viewing field of the meter will be consistent to the field of illumination. Remember — the field of view of meters such as the Weston V is about 30°; the meter must be used at a distance where its field lies *within* the borders of the card, otherwise erroneous readings will obtain.

33

In order to insure consistent results, the exposure meter should be placed in a fixed position to the card and carefully shielded from any direct light from the reflectors. Unless the meter is very sensitive, it may be necessary to use the white side of the test card. In any case, adjust the distance of light-to-subject so that the readings are around 6.5 c/ft^2; very low values may not be accurately indicated or easily read. With the S.E.I. Meter, brightness values can be measured with great accuracy and the "reading" distance is not an important factor. The card should be evenly illuminated.

The relative efficiency of the various reflectors used under the above fixed conditions is simply indicated by the relative brightness readings of the test card. Note these values in your permanent record book.

Next, direct the reflectors to a large even-toned surface, such as a light wall. Study the distribution of light within the field of illumination of the reflector. If the field of illumination is irregular in intensity, if "circles" of different illumination value show, or if there is a visible "hot spot," the reflector is suspect. With a good brushed aluminum reflector and a well-centered lamp, the field of illumination should be continuous and of equal value over a considerable area. Of course the brightness of the field will diminish toward its boundaries due to a natural falling off of the illumination from the reflector. (See Fig. 29a, page 55.)

Some reflectors of strong curvature or cone shape are designed to throw a small field of illumination. It is advisable to note in your record book the approximate angle of the efficient illumination field of each reflector, and (if you are using an S.E.I. Meter) to note the brightnesses at different angles of coverage from the axis.

Also test for the relative values of diffusing devices you may use over the reflectors. Identify every device and make accurate notes. To test the reflectors for efficiency, refer to page 40.

Flashlamps

Flashlamps and speedlamps, are, in effect, "packaged light." Knowing the luminous output of any flashlamp or speedlamp, we can calculate exposures to a high degree of accuracy, and "place" subject values precisely where we wish on the exposure scale if we know the relative reflectances of the subject. We can estimate these reflectances by interpolation of "steady-burning" lights or, for less precise results, we can employ the neutral gray card as a "pivot" value. The Inverse Square Law holds as with ordinary light. Flashlamps come in both tungsten and daylight quality; speedlamps are of daylight quality, and color filters may be used as with daylight and/or tungsten illumination.

The chief difficulty in using flash lies in visualizing the effects of the light on the subject—the modeling, shadow and highlight disposition, etc. Hence, the use of "finding" or "modeling" lights in conjunction with the flashlamps is imperative for positive compositional results. Reference is made to the lighting fixture described in Book 1, page 66; a two-circuit system in which ordinary lamps serve as modeling lights (and which should be on a "dim" switch so that their power can be reduced when the flashlamps are fired). Many of the speedlamps have a modeling light circuit built into their reflector units. As will be discussed later on, the *relative* power of the modeling lights and the flashlamps must be the same, otherwise the balance of lighting will not be as desired.

34

23. In the Library (Eastman School of Music, Rochester, New York). Made with a 4x5 view camera and a 5-inch lens; camera back severely tilted to bring near portion of book and girl's head into the focal plane. It was necessary to stop to f/22 to gain all-over sharpness. This demonstrates the "near-far" compositional approach. The lighting was simple—one light in a broad reflector over the girl's head, which illuminated her hair, hand, and the pages of the large book; another light (about one-fourth the intensity of the first light) was directed from the right, providing most of the illumination on the face. Reflection from the book pages also threw light into the face, and simulated the "reality" of the light in the library room.

When we have determined what equipment we will need (acquire equipment with caution until actual needs are known), the first step should be the evaluation of output of light from the flashlamps *as applied to our equipment and our personal lighting requirements and taste.*

Tests for Flashlamp Values

We are now ready to proceed with the very important tests which will give us full command of flash exposure. Again it is advised that these tests be made with the greatest possible accuracy; they are very important, and once the basic values are established and clearly recorded, subsequent additions and refinement can be made by comparison and interpolation. *It is not necessary to test for all lamps in all reflectors.*

Small "midget" flashlamps should be tested in their appropriate reflectors. However, the small lamps can be used in large reflectors if the lamp is centered in the same position as the center of the larger lamps; their effective light output will then be in approximate proportion to their rated luminosity.

One basic test should provide most of the information required:

1. Set up the gray card in a fixed position out of doors at night, in a low-reflectance environment, or in a large dark-walled room.

2. Place the card so that it is at about 45° to the axis of the lens and/or the direction of the light. This is to avoid glare. (See Fig. 20, page 30.)

3. The light may be directly over or close to the axis of the camera.

4. Use a standard camera and lens and load the holders with the type of film to be used generally. (With roll film, one roll can be devoted to each basic test; the entire roll, being developed as one unit, assures accurate comparative results.)

5. Select a standard flashlamp, say a G.E. No. 11, and a standard diffused-surface reflector (such as was considered "standard" in previous tests with regular lamps).

6. Note the manufacturer's recommended guide numbers for open flash (1/25 second or longer), and base the tests on this guide number as a start. Let us assume this guide number is 240 with a tungsten film speed of 64. If the light is 11 feet from the card, the lens stop indicated is f/22 (guide number ÷ distance-to-subject = lens stop). Convenient round figures may be used.

7. Make the following exposures (with the same flashlamps and no change in the setup).

		Approximate Guide Number Values
1	f/11	120
2	f/11-16 (f/12.5)	140
3	f/16	175
4	f/16-22 (f/18)	200
5	f/22	240 (mfg. rating)
6	f/22-32 (f/25)	275
7	f/32	350

If the test card is close to the lens (watch for shadows of camera, hands, etc., on the card), and the lens is extended beyond its infinity focal setting, do not fail to calculate the lens-extension exposure factor (see page viii). A smooth test image will obtain if the lens is at infinity focal setting, but operated close to the test card; the card will be thoroughly out of focus and textures eliminated, but no extension factor is required.

8. Suppose that with daylight or steady-burning lamps our "normal" negative shows a density of 0.9 above film base-fog density for a Zone V exposure (or 1.1 for a Zone VI exposure); we know that any subject-brightness placed on Zone V of the exposure scale and developed for normal development time (for the particular film used) will yield a density of 0.9 (above film base-fog), or a density of 1.1 for a Zone VI placement. Let us assume that 0.9 is the density we wish to obtain for the negative image of the gray card (Zone V brightness value) in these tests. But here we are using a gray card of known reflectance (18 per cent); we do not measure its brightness, since its "brightness" exists only during the flash exposure. We are working to discover how to get a Zone V value in the negative from a Zone V surface by exposing with flashlamp illumination. Now develop all of the above 7 negatives for the standard "normal" developing time being careful to immerse, agitate, and remove all films together. (Refer to Book 2.)

9. When dry, measure the negatives on a densitometer.

The negative which shows a density of 0.9 for the gray card image will be the key to the optimum guide number. Should no negative have the exact desired value, the one closest to the desired value will suggest a close approximation of the guide number. It is then advisable to make another test—3 negatives "bracketing" the close example.

10. Suppose we find that negative Number 3 has the desired density value. The effective guide number would then be 175 (lens stop f/16 x distance 11 feet = guide number 175); if negative Number 2 has the desired density, the guide number would be 140. This guide number can be considered basic for the *particular camera film, lamp and reflector* used. How can we determine the proper guide numbers for other lamps, other shutter speeds, for other film and for other reflectors? The procedure is outlined below.

Before we proceed, it is necessary to be very sure that the significance and character of guide numbers has been grasped. As the guide numbers relate to the lens stops, and as the lens stops are geometric numbers, the guide numbers are also geometric. That is, double the value of the guide number and you obtain 4 times the intensity of the light. This represents a difference of 2 stops. A lamp with a guide number of 100 has 1/4 the intensity of a lamp with a guide number of 200. Confusion persists when we use higher or lower guide numbers for the same lamp when we wish to place subject-brightnesses on different zones of the exposure scale. Reference to the table below and page 38 will show that, in order to "place" a given subject on any zone of the scale, we must organize our guide numbers in a definite geometric progression. When we wish to increase a guide number by 1 stop (2x light intensity), we must multiply the basic guide number by 1.4 (this is approximately the square root of 2). If we wish to increase a guide number by 1/2 stop (1½x light intensity, or 3/4 exposure value for the same lamp) we multiply the basic guide number by 1.2. The resulting figures are not *exact*, but adequate for practical work.

Guide numbers for various Zone placements.

Zones:	I	II	III	IV	V	VI	VII	VIII	IX	X
	720	500	360	250	180	125	90	60	45	30

Note that *every other* guide number doubles or halves in value; the numbers in between are related to the preceding or following numbers by a factor of about 1.4.

This table means that if you wish to place a Zone V brightness value on Zone VIII, you would use a guide number of 60. (60 ÷ 11 ft. = f/5.6.) Obviously, this stop gives a *greater* exposure value than would f/16 (which would "place" a Zone V brightness on Zone V of the scale). Further, if you desired a Zone III placement of the Zone V brightness value, you would use a guide number of 360. (360 ÷ 11 ft. = f/32). Obviously, this stop gives a *lesser* exposure value than would f/16 (which would "place" a Zone V brightness on Zone V of the scale).

The smaller the guide number, the larger the lens stop indicated, and the *more* exposure for any particular lamp.

If a guide number places a Zone V brightness on Zone V of the exposure scale (and thereby results in the normal negative density for such placement and exposure), *it automatically places all other subject brightnesses on their proper Zone of the Exposure Scale.*

Hence, if we wish to place a Zone VI brightness on Zone VI, we do not arbitrarily use the guide number which appears under Zone IV of the above scale. The guide number 180 relates to *all* zones for this *particular* lamp and film: so if we wish to place *any* value 2 zones lower on the scale, we must select the guide number *2 zones lower from the position of 180*. This would be 360.

Do not attempt calculations until this is clearly understood. It is very simple once it is firmly grasped.

The chart below will show the effective guide numbers for placement of various brightnesses on different zones of the scale. The guide number 180 is used throughout; the same principle would apply to any basic guide number.

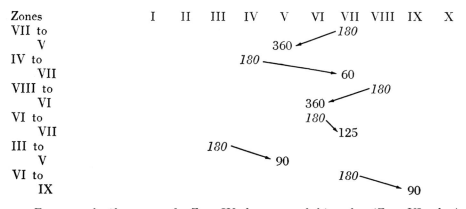

For example, if we wanted a Zone IV placement of skin value (Zone VI value) we would use the guide number 360, which would yield 1/4 normal exposure. If we wanted a Zone VI placement of a Zone VII value, we would use the Guide Number 250.

Guide Numbers for Other Flashlamps

We may assume that the manufacturers' guide numbers for their lamps are consistent, and it would therefore hold that the ratio between our personally determined guide number and the manufacturer's number for a particular lamp would be the same for other lamps used *under the same conditions*. Hence, we may calculate the effective personal guide number of any lamp by the simple proportion formula. For example, if the listed guide number for our first test lamp is 220, and we find that our personal guide number for it is 180; then if we wish to use a lamp of a listed rating of 400, what would be the relative personal guide number for it? The formula is simply this:

$$220 : 180 :: 400 : x$$
$$180 \text{ x } 400 = 72,000$$
$$72,000 \div 220 = 327$$

(330 in round numbers; 320 would be close enough for practical purposes.)

Hence we can make up a table of Zone placements for this guide number as follows:

Zones:	I	II	III	IV	V	VI	VII	VIII	IX	X
	1280	900	640	450	320	225	160	115	80	55

It is important to repeat here that when the midget lamps are used, a separate test should be made for them in the special reflectors designed for their use. However, provided that the center of the peanut lamp corresponds with the center of the larger lamps used when positioned in the large reflectors, the relative values when used with these larger reflectors can be approximated by reference to the manufacturer's data on the total *luminous output* of the lamp.

Remember, *do not* mix the geometric guide numbers and the arithmetical luminous output values in the same proportion formula! If the Press 40 has 40,000 lumen-seconds output, and the G-E Synchro-Press No. 5 has 16,000 lumen-seconds, we can assume that the output of the latter lamp is less than half that of the Press 40. The personal guide number therefore would be about 120 (assuming 180 as the basic guide number). This guide number would serve as a close approximation of actual value—at least as the basis for a few "bracketing" tests of the small lamp in the large reflector.

Guide Numbers for Various Shutter Speeds

It is not feasible to determine the relative guide numbers for various shutter speeds by calculating on the basis of the shutter speeds themselves. (Remember, the *stated* speed of a shutter is one thing, and the *actual* speed another! Have your shutter tested frequently and calculate on the actual speeds delivered. It will often be found that a shutter marked 1/200 actually yields 1/100, and a 1/400 setting actually yields about 1/200.) The first tests were based on "open flash," which utilizes all of the light from the lamp. (See paragraph 6, page 36.)

Different lamps have different characteristics of peak intensity, duration of flash, etc. We should rely on the guide numbers *provided by the manufacturer* and obtain our personal guide number for various shutter speeds by proportionate calculation. If, for example, the manufacturer's guide number for a given lamp with open flash was 200 and our personal guide number for the same lamp was 160 —if the listed guide number for the lamp at 1/200 second was 130, what would our personal guide number be for it at that shutter speed?

39

The formula is: 200 : 160 :: 130 x
                    160 x 130 = 20,800
                    20,800 ÷ 200 = 104
                    (100 in round figures)

A table of placements for this guide number would be:

Zones	I	II	III	IV	V	VI	VII	VIII	IX	X
Lamp A @ 1/200 sec.										
with reflector B....	400	280	200	140	100	70	50	35	25	18

Guide Numbers for Different Film

Again, refer to the listed guide numbers for both the film you are using and other negative material; then calculate the relative personal guide number by the proportion formula which follows: Suppose the listed rating of a given lamp is 200 for film of Weston 32, and our personal guide number is 160—and that the manufacturer's rating for the same lamp for Weston rating 64 is 280: what would our personal guide number be for it?

$$200 : 160 :: 280 : x$$
$$160 \times 280 = 44,800$$
$$44,800 \div 200 = 224$$
(220 in round figures)

A table of placements for this guide number would be:

	I	II	III	IV	V	VI	VII	VIII	IX	X
Open flash										
with film speed	880	600	440	300	220	150	110	75	55	40

Guide Numbers for Various Reflectors

A carefully prepared table should be made up which lists the relative efficiency of various reflectors, and this can be applied to the use of flashlamps as well as floodlamps. However, the values in the table, being arithmetic, cannot be used together with the geometric guide numbers in the same formula. Therefore, if we based our first tests on reflector A, with reflector B the output would be 1.5x greater. To increase the effective value of a guide number about 1.5x, we must multiply the geometric number by *1.2* (to be exact 1.225). If our personal guide number for a given lamp is 180 in reflector A, with reflector B it would be 180x1.2, or 216 (220 in round numbers).

A table of placements for this guide number would be:

Lamp C in Ref. B	I	II	III	IV	V	VI	VII	VIII	IX	X
Open flash	880	600	440	300	220	150	110	75	55	40

For reflector C (.75 efficiency compared with reflector A), we will *divide* 180 by 1.2: the answer is 150. A table of Zone placements for this guide number is as follows:

Lamp C in Ref. C	I	II	III	IV	V	VI	VII	VIII	IX	X
Open flash	600	440	300	200	150	110	75	55	40	25

For practical purposes, approximation of other factors indicated in this table can be made by "judgment." Precise values are desirable in *computation*, but the variables of equipment and materials—even the best—indicate that there is not a need for *exact* values. For example, if the efficiency of reflector A is 1 and that of reflector B is 1.5, and the relative effective guide numbers are 180 and 220 respectively, we can assume that a reflector (efficiency of 1.25) would represent a guide number of about 200. Such approximations are sufficiently close for all practical purposes.

The reader may wonder if there is a contradiction between this statement and previous admonitions on accuracy in other parts of this book. I believe we should be as exact as possible in theory, and determine our basic values as *precisely* as possible. Remember, *errors can accumulate!* On the other hand, when we come to a practical application of determined values, we should be sensible and allow for the many variations inherent in shutters, film and developers.

Preparation of Reference Tables

From the foregoing the reader will see that he can produce adequate working tables relating to his lighting equipment, and that these tables are sufficiently accurate for practical photography. He can utilize the Exposure Record* for these tables, placing the basic guide number under Zone V.

Speedlights

The advantages of the speedlights are obvious: thousands of flashes from a single tube (thereby avoiding the annoyance of lamp replacement after each exposure), light of daylight quality (7000°K), and extremely short duration of flash (1/500 to 1/10,000 second or less in commercial models). However, except for very large models, the actual light output of speedlights is less than with average flashlamps. Coverage of large areas is therefore not feasible with the common types of speedlights. Speedlights may be operated from both line current and batteries; some pieces of equipment may be used with either type of power, while others are limited to batteries alone. Reference is made here to the Photo-Lab-Index, Section 10, for detailed information on speedlights and flashlamps, their relative powers and illumination characteristics, etc. Of prime importance to the photographer are the exposure characteristics of speedlamps; the high color temperature (7000 °K) is quite bluish and demands more than normal development of the negative (blue light scatters more and penetrates less through the emulsion than does light of longer wavelengths).

Guide numbers for speedlights are established in the same manner as for flash, *except* that the efficient guide numbers for speedlights alone will be higher than for speedlights used in conjunction with daylight; with the latter we must develop for the daylight components of the scene, whereas for speedlights alone we can give normal-plus development to overcome the flattening effect of the bluish color of the light, and take advantage of higher film speeds. However, we must be on guard against increase of grain in the negative which additional development may cause.

---

*Exposure Record, *by Ansel Adams*, Morgan & Morgan, Inc., New York. If he wishes, he can place the basic guide number under Zone VI, or any other Zone of the exposure scale. However, he should be consistent in this throughout. Once these tables are completed they will serve to provide immediate information of great value to the practicing photographer.

24. Dr. Dexter Perkins, Historian. This is an example of a fairly sharp "bounce" light; a No. 4 Photoflood in a deep cone reflector was directed onto a light-toned ceiling, producing a brilliant circle of light about 15 inches across. *(Warning:* Do not allow hot lamps to burn at full energy near walls, ceilings, curtains, etc., because severe damage may result, to say nothing of the general fire hazard. Use a Hi-Lo switch when composing, turning it to *High* just before the exposure is made.) The small circle of illumination produced rather sharp shadow edges and highlights; relatively short exposure and normal-plus development increased the brilliancy of the image. A "catchlight" lamp would have added sparkle to the eyes. Reflection of the circle of light on the ceiling is caught in the glasses on the book.

"Bounced" light is illumination directed to the subject from a relatively large surface on which light from the light source is concentrated, such as a pale wall or ceiling, a large white card, a sheet, etc. This surface should have a high but diffuse reflectance. Glossy surfaces do not serve well, as they reflect the bounce light in a rather narrow beam.

Diffuse light reflected from a ceiling, wall, card, or sheet reflects in all directions, whereas light from a high-gloss surface would reflect at the "glare" angle. Hence the total amount of bounce light falling upon the subject is proportionally less than the light from the source itself when directed on the subject. In any situation this ratio can be determined by comparative brightness readings; the author has not found any practical "rule of thumb" to meet all situations. The surface quality, as well as the reflectance, of the bounce area must be considered.

In testing for the relative illumination value of bounced light in relation to a standard lamp reflector, we should place the bounce reflecting surface at the same distance from the test card as the lamp reflector was placed in the earlier tests. First turn the light on the test card and take a reading; then direct the light against the bounce surface and take another reading of the card. The readings will indicate the relative illumination value of the bounce surface to that of the direct light from the lamp—in other words, its effective reflectance.

Two important facts are to be noted:

1. Provided *all* of the projected light from the light source is "confined" within the limits of the diffuse reflecting surface, the distance of the light source from this surface does not affect the total amount of "bounce" light to the subject. The *reflecting-surface-to-subject distance*, however, is subject to the Inverse Square Law. The light source should be preferably in a deep cone reflector (a spotlight is better), as the light should not scatter but should be fully directed to the reflecting surface. It is also advisable to have as large a "bounce" surface as possible. A moment's thought about this will clarify the point; if all the light from a reflector is concentrated in a circle 2 feet in diameter, we may say that a given *volume* of light is so concentrated. If we move the light source away from the reflecting surface so that the circle of illumination is 3 feet in diameter, the same *volume* of light exists in the 3-foot circle as existed in the 2-foot one and the *amount* of light reflected from the bounce surface is the same in either case. The brightness of each unit of area of the 3-foot circle is less than the brightness of a similar unit in the 2-foot circle, but the area of the 3-foot circle is larger. In both cases, all of the light source is projected to the bounce surface and then reflected to the subject, modified only by the reflectance of the bounce surface. (See Figs. 24, 25 and 55.) Of course, as the reflectance of the bounce surface is reduced, the light output therefrom is less: a wall surface of 80 per cent reflectance bounces 80 per cent of the light falling upon it, and a wall of 20 per cent reflectance bounces just 1/5 of that amount.

2. The size of the circle of illumination on the bounce surface modifies the *quality* of the bounced light on the subject; the larger the circle of illumination, the broader the light on the subject. Softer highlights and shadow edges obtain. Textures are minimized. This fact may be demonstrated by placing the gray card and some object (such as a piece of sculpture) in a fixed position on table or floor surface and directing a cone reflector on a light ceiling or other bounce surface.

Bringing the reflector as close to the bounce surface as possible, we will note a certain brightness value of the gray card and a certain quality of highlight and shadow edge on the object. As we increase the distance of the cone reflector from the bounce surface, we will note a softening of highlight and shadow edge in the object (since the circle of illumination is larger), but there is no appreciable difference in the brightness value of the gray card.

The actual brightness of the shadows depends upon the "environmental" light —that is, the light reflected from walls, floors, and furnishings. If these are of high reflectance, the shadows will be of higher value than would obtain from dark walls, rugs, etc. If we were operating in a room with a light ceiling and very dark walls we would find our image would be surprisingly harsh, even with a large bounce area used. The environmental reflections do not appreciably affect the brightnesses of the higher values (Zone VI and up, see page 28.)

When working with bounced light, we must be very careful not to obscure any of the light by the lamp reflector itself. The surface used for the bounce light should be smooth for the most even illumination. A specular surface (tin foil, for example) will put out more light at the angle of reflection as it reflects the beam in one narrow direction, but it may also give rather harsh effects in both highlights and shadow values, simulating the qualities of direct light rather than a diffuse "shadow" illumination.

Recapitulation

1. In daylight, or with steady-burning light, we measure the brightness of any surface and place this brightness at will on the exposure scale. We can change the effective negative densities of higher values by development control with relatively small alteration of the low values. The important thing to remember is that we measure *all* brightnesses of a subject as they appear before the camera.

2. With flashlamp illumination we cannot make direct evaluation of subject brightnesses before exposure, for obvious reasons. So how do we *know* how much flash to use to get the desired results? We will make the first tests on a subject of *known* reflectance, such as the gray card (18 per cent reflectance), and consider that amount of development "normal" which will give a negative density of, say, 0.9 above film base-fog density for this subject exposed on Zone V.

3. Through a series of test exposures (based on the manufacturer's recommendations for the particular film and lamp used), we will find the proper exposure for our equipment which will give the required density with "normal" development time. This optimum exposure is stated in terms of a Guide Number.

4. If our optimum Guide Number is 220, related stops and lamp-to-subject distance would be (in round figures):

f/8	28 feet
f/11	20 feet
f/16	14 feet
f/22	10 feet
f/32	7 feet
f/45	5 feet

5. All of the exposures above would be, of course, identical in value and would represent an 18 per cent reflectant surface (Zone V) of the subject as a negative density of 0.9 (Zone V negative value). This in turn would print a Zone V

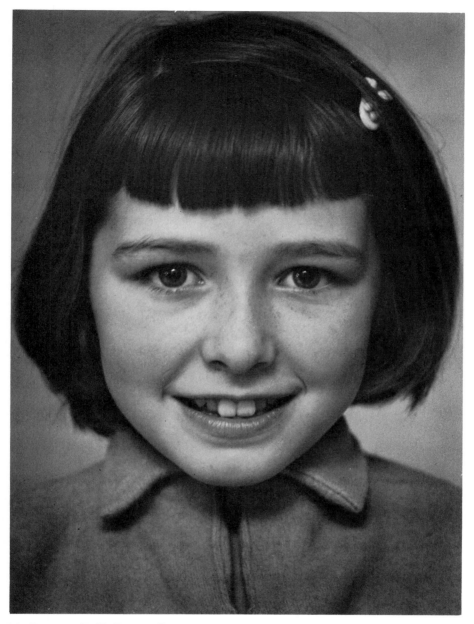

25. Portrait, Child; Bounce Light. This was made with Hasselbad Camera, 135mm Kodak Ektar Lens. Figure was posed in a rather small room with light walls and ceiling. A 1000-watt lamp in a large "bowl" reflector was directed to the ceiling; the light on the subject was soft, and there was a "natural" fall-off of light on the background wall (which, fortunately, produced the appropriate tone for the background). The shade was removed from a conventional stand lamp, and this provided the catchlights in the eyes. The light was fairly strong and the exposure about 1/10 second. Development was normal-plus to increase brilliancy and texture.

gray when the film-base-plus-fog density of the negative is rendered as a maximum black in the print.

6. All other subject zones would be rendered in their appropriate densities. Therefore, when making flash exposures we can if necessary estimate the contrast of the image by measuring the brightness of the various areas of the subject under a steady-burning light, and this *ratio* will be of help in determining the desired amount of development that should be given the negative—or will assist us in the relative positioning of 2 or more lights.

7. If we have an obviously low-contrast subject, we can drop the general placement one or two Zones (if our basic guide number is 220, using guide numbers of 300 or 440) and develop normal-plus-1 or normal-plus-2.

8. Many failures in flash photography may be traced to careless evaluation of shadow values; if the flash is on the lens axis, all reflectances of the subject will be recorded within the exposure scale. If the flash is to one side of the camera, we will have to contend with shadows; these can be controlled by reflecting screens or by the use of secondary flash (preferably bounced light from an ample surface).

9. In testing for speedlights, we follow the same basic procedure. However, due to the extremely short duration of the light (and high color temperature), the reciprocity effect requires that we prolong development to 1.5 or 2x "normal" for daylight and tungsten light. Tests are therefore made with this prolonged development in mind.

However, when we use speedlights for fill-in lights with daylight pictures (see page 28 and Book 2, page 94), development times must relate to *daylight* exposure. Hence, separate tests for the personal guide numbers should be made for normal daylight developing times, as well as tests for the speedlights when used alone. An approximate example would be: if a guide number for speedlights used alone was 350 for 1.5 normal development, the guide number for synchro-sunlight work would be about 220 for normal development times. We must also remember to think of *daylight* film speeds when working with speedlights.

10. When working with tungsten light or regular flashlamps used in conjunction with daylight (sunlight or skylight coming through door or window, or exterior scene viewed through door or window, etc.), we must remember that the illumination values and exposures are based on tungsten speed ratings, and that areas illuminated by daylight will receive 1/4 to 1/3 *more* exposure in proportion to their measured brightnesses than will areas under tungsten or flash illumination. As we can seldom control daylight, we will need to increase the tungsten or flash illumination by 1/4 or 1/3 its calculated value—and then give the exposure as determined by the daylight brightnesses. Or, when balancing artificial light with daylight, we can use *blue* flood or flashlamps. (This is imperative in color photography, unless special unrealistic effects are desired.)

Many of the errors which occur in photography can be traced to the simple omission of details of calculations and procedure. The photographer must always be in a questioning mood: "Have I set the meter to the right film speed? Have I figured the lens extension? Did I measure the distance of the light *after* changing its position on the subject? Have I entered the brightnesses in their proper columns of the Exposure Record?, etc. A check-off list will help to avoid such accidents, which can easily turn out to be major disasters! It is advisable to group the various operations under "camera," "lights," "film," etc.

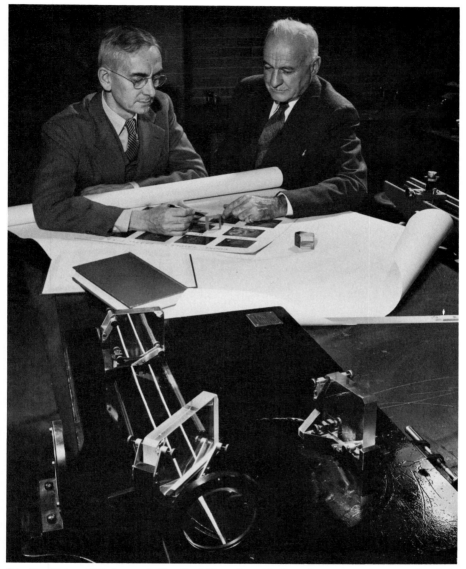

26. Dr. Brian O'Brien and Mr. Carl Bausch, with Interferometer. An example of the "near-far" compositional approach; the foreground apparatus was only about 15 inches from the lens. The picture was made with a 4x5 view camera and a 5-inch lens; the camera back and lens board were severely tilted to establish adequate depth of field, and the lens stopped to f/32 for all-over clarity. One top light illuminated the man on the right and the papers on the table. Another light from the left illuminated the faces. A strong light from the far right built up the illumination on the foreground apparatus which, however, presented a real difficulty. The bed of the interferometer was jet black (the bright reflection on the far right shows this). A more central lighting would only have aggravated the reflections. To show this jet black, glossy surface with a suggestion of *substance* would have required a light card or fabric suspended overhead from which a broad "bounce" light could be utilized.

27. Interior, Office. This room, as well as the furniture, was veneered with warm-toned red-wood; the chairs were in a soft leather and the floor a quiet fabric of related values. The illumination was mostly from the recessed ceiling with, of course, a little light from the window. A broad floodlight was directed from the wall on the left (somewhat behind the camera), and this illuminated the back of the foreground chair and the front of the desk. The soft shadows from this light can be seen on the floor. The general contrast of the subject was very low; "expanded" development was indicated. Accordingly, water-bath development was applied (the 2-solution development would not be used), with more than normal time of immersion in the developer solution. Because shadow values needed "building up," and there was some texture to be preserved in the brilliant window, a straight normal-plus development was not used. The water-bath or 2-solution processes can be used when increased brilliancy is desired; the effect is somewhat different from that obtained from regular extended development; more "separation" and body in the shadows (in reference to high-value texture) will be obtained. This plate is reproduced from a "work print," and there has been no control over window and ceiling values. A good print would show certain differences—better window and ceiling detail, and richer values in the lower left corner.

48

APPLICATIONS OF ARTIFICIAL LIGHT

In the following pages a variety of applications and problems will be treated in a more or less basic way. The object is not to go into exhaustive details, but to point out certain facts and procedures which will help the serious student in his search for a dependable approach and technique. In any exposition of this general nature, there is always the danger of suggesting fixed and final procedures and styles. This is definitely not my intention; these statements are meant to stimulate a variety of thought, experiment and application.

Interiors

The control of illumination on small objects, of course, is much simpler than on large objects in large volumes of space. But in every case the inexorable Inverse Square Law troubles us, and the placement of lights to assure balanced illumination and avoid obvious distortions of highlights and shadow requires observation and study of both visual and metered values.

When we walk into a room, we are conscious of a certain *reality of light.* Or, we might say, we are conscious of the *effects* of light—not necessarily of the light sources themselves. To interpret this *"existing"* quality of illumination is a supreme test of photographic abilities. In the majority of photographs of architecture, the mood and atmosphere of the subject appears secondary to the physical aspects of its structure and decor and the photographer is tempted to overlight his subject, both in volume and direction of the lighting. More often than not, theatrical effects are produced; these effects, while relatively exciting in a superficial way, may not interpret the subject as it is in actual experience. We are concerned here with realistic problems and not with exotic effects. It is wise to recall that the eye adapts itself to a tremendous range of brightnesses—far beyond the capacity of the uncontrolled photographic image to record.

The average interior presents a very wide range of subject-brightnesses. If we photograph by the existing light alone, we will usually find the results much too harsh, and false to the original mood. If we flood the interior with light, we will in all probability create an equally false impression. Through visualization, we have the means for a satisfactory interpretation of the subject before us. The procedure is as follows:

1. Visualize the final print in terms of desired black-and-white values, which represent the important brightnesses of the subject. In other words, think of the darkest area in which you want detail to show as a Zone II value, and the lightest area in which you want texture to show as a Zone VIII value. (Light sources and specular reflections would fall on Zone IX and above.) Certain very dark "pockets" of shadow might be visualized as solid black without tonal variation or texture.

2. The object is to apply light so that the *actual* brightness range will approximate the *visualized* range. There is marked difference between the *visual* and the *visualized!* And between the *visual* and the *metered* values! This statement represents the fundamental justification for the Zone System approach.

3. We will first take a meter reading of the existing brightnesses; let us say that the darkest area in which we wish texture to appear (Zone II placement) registers 0.1 c/ft², and the brightest area registers 100 c/ft². The existing brightness range is 1:1,000 (II to XII). The optimum brightness range should be about 1:64 (II to VII).

4. We can assume that the brightest existing diffuse value can be utilized and placed on Zone VIII. That necessitates the addition of sufficient light to raise the Zone II values to 1.6 c/ft^2 brightness.

Let us assume that we will illuminate the scene so as to achieve the desired brightness range. For the sake of simplicity, let us use but one enveloping light, which will add a consistent amount of illumination to the entire subject. As we desire the brightness of 100 to fall on Zone VIII, we will have to add sufficient light to produce a brightness of 1.6 on Zone II. Below is the original brightness range which will suggest the amount of illumination required to assure the correct brightness range.

	I	II	III	IV	V	VI	VII	VIII	IX	X	XI	XII	XIII	XIX
Existing	0.1	.2	.4	.8	1.6	3.2	6.5	13	25	50	100			

If we place the highest value on Zone VIII

.8	1.6	3.2	6.5	13	25	50	100

obviously all values below .8 will be recorded as total black, and the image will be a very different thing from what the eye "sees." Accordingly we will add enough light to render the darkest part of the subject on Zone II; all proportionally *reflective* areas will fall into their appropriate Zones. However, this implies that the added light only *augments* the existing light—it must be of the same quality of diffusion and direction! If the light is of different quality and comes from a different direction, there will probably be a great change in the general effect; shadows will be so illuminated that they lose their "shadow" quality, etc., and the total effect may be one of quite different feeling from that inherent in the subject under normal existing light.

The term "enveloping" light as used above needs a little clarification. It may be produced by a soft axis light, bounce light from the ceiling, bounce light from the walls, or any of these in combination. It is not a *directional* light, and is used to augment the character of the existing light. Shadows are not created—at least to an extent which would hint of applied directional lighting. On the other hand, it will usually be necessary to "expand" and subtly exaggerate the existing values. Rules cannot be made; each problem demands its own solution.

One method of solving the problem would be to expose frankly with the existing light—placing the darkest important value in which detail is required on Zone II and controlling the high values as much as possible by special development of the negative (2-solution, Pyrocatechin, etc). However, these methods cannot yield truly satisfactory textural qualities in the high values.

To recapitulate, we observe and study the subject visually; then visualize the completed print. Next, with care and devotion to basic visualized impression, we add sufficient light or lights to bring all the values of the subject into the desired range—but still preserving the original *impression* of the subject under its existing illumination. Once the image is visualized, the values can be entered on the Exposure Record, first in terms of Zone *placements* for the important elements of the subject, and then in terms of the actual brightness values required. When the photograph is planned in this way, the illumination can be manipulated so as to achieve the desired brightnesses.

Adding sufficient illumination to raise the lower values to the desired brightness will, of course, add some light to the higher values, but this increase will be inconsequential. (See page 28).

50

To repeat: we cannot trust our eyes to judge brightness differences accurately. Nor can we overlook the possible reciprocity effect with long exposures (page 4). Careful use of an adequate brightness meter provides the only positive control*

Almost without exception, the intensity of illumination in a room should *increase* in relation to distance from the camera. If the lighting of all planes is of equal intensity, a dismal flatness and lack of "space feeling" will result. If the lighting on the nearer planes is more intense than on the further planes, a disturbing sense of emptiness and bleak space may obtain. Of course, planes and objects within the field may be emphasized, but the foregoing refers to *general* lighting of an interior subject.

Scale

In photographing complex subjects such as interiors, we should consider the problem of relative scale versus exaggerated scale of objects, and also the importance of having the entire photograph "read" clearly. The problem of scale is of great importance and always perplexing. When we visually scan a room, the eye travels about freely and the impressions of the room are quite unlike any impression that could be literally compressed within the confines of the print. To increase the scope of the picture we frequently use a wide-angle lens. This, of course, effectively reduces the size of the objects and expands the field of view. The result is usually one of remoteness, distorted space-and-form relationships, and confusion of scale. If we inject a relatively small, near object into the field of view, we will partially establish an impression of space and scale; the obvious difference between the size of the near small object (rendered large) and the distant spaces of the room (rendered small) will give us a spacial orientation. The near object is physically within reach. This "departure from reality" actually intensifies the impression of reality—whereas the image of the room alone might convey no acute impression of space or scale. If a long lens is used, only a part of the room can be shown; this may have a more truthful literal impact on the spectator, but might not contain sufficient area and "information" to please the client! The problem is interpretive as well as informative, and can be attacked both by use of proper lenses, and by appropriate distribution of illumination. Figure 28 is a good example of the use of the "near-far" approach to interior photography.

By "reading clearly" we mean that not only the merging of brightness values should be avoided, but that confusing juxtapositions of form and line, and the obscuring of one object by another, be carefully eliminated in composing the image. To be certain of precise organization of subject details, we must observe the subject from the position of the lens; standing even a foot or so on either side of the lens may give an inaccurate impression of what the lens is actually seeing. We must take nothing for granted; we must examine every line and edge to see how it "follows through" without confusion with other elements in the picture. Such careful organization of detail provides one of the most important "convictions" of creative photography.

---

*I am fully aware that my constant reference to a refined and sensitive brightness meter such as the S.E.I. will probably distress many a student reader and practicing photographer on economic grounds. The meter is a rather expensive one. Actually—especially with color work—it will pay for itself many times over, in material terms alone. The acquisition of such a meter is earnestly advised; in my opinion *it is almost as vital as the camera and lens* in the practice of serious photography.

Subject connotations play an important part in expressive photography. For example, we enter a tastefully decorated modern room. On the table reposes a fine piece of abstract sculpture; it is in key with the room as a whole, and relates to other examples of contemporary art therein. A strictly "informational" wide-range picture would show a large part of the room and many of the objects of art *in situ*. Now, we "move in" on the piece of sculpture on the table, exaggerating its relative size (the "near-far" principle) to give space and "scale" to the room. The sculpture now becomes important, and its mood may dominate the mood of the room. Employing exaggerated lighting on the sculpture would further intensify its dominance; the spectator would relate the connotations of the sculpture to the room as a whole. An object—originally only a part of an organized whole—now becomes the dominant, controlling center of attention; the photograph is of a work of art in a favorable environment, rather than of a room-as-a-whole in which works of art are placed. The same "near-far" effect might be retained while reducing the dominance of the sculpture by low-key lighting or applying a semi-silhouette treatment, etc. The photographer must evaluate the relative significance of objects as well as their intrinsic qualities of brightness, form, and physical relation to the subject as a whole.

28. Interior (courtesy, Fritz Baldauf, designer). An example of the "near-far" approach in interior composition. The plant, actually within 3 feet from the lens, does not possess a definite scale or connotation, yet it contributes to the impression of space and depth. The lighting was chiefly "bounce" light from the ceiling (a small circle of light), placed so as to just strike the knobs of the desk drawers and throw them into relief. A second light was "bounced" from the wall on the extreme right (out of the picture). The table lamp was turned on for about 1/3 of the total exposure. A view camera was used and carefully leveled. The back side-swing was used to correct the focal plane from the near plane to the distant wall.

While multiple lights may solve an illumination problem, they usually produce a complex shadow effect which is very difficult to overcome. The ideal arrangement is to show a single shadow effect (implying one general light source) and to employ a broad "fill-in" light to achieve a satisfactory level of illumination throughout the image. We are all familiar with the disturbing effect of multiple shadows (and multiple highlights as well) which suggest the presence of many lights. In the ideal photograph one should never be conscious of the lights employed in making it. In a small room it may be possible to use one broad light as the main source of illumination and add a general "bounce" light from walls and/or ceiling. In this way only one shadow effect would result, and if the direction of the main light coincided with a window or a light fixture this effect would appear quite logical. A "quiet" room will often photograph harshly, with more black "empty" spaces than visually observed. This is because, as our eyes scan a subject, they automatically adjust for brightness differences; the lens does not!

One of the most aggravating problems in the use of artificial light is overcoming the inevitable effects of the Inverse Square Law—the progressive diminution of intensity as the distance of light-to-subject increases. (Intensity decreases as the *square* of the distance increases.) It is especially troublesome in photographing interiors and large objects where the size of the object—or volume in space—is considerable in relation to the restricted distance of the light. For example, if we are photographing a piece of furniture at 15 feet from the light, and the wall of the room is 10 feet beyond, the ratio of light intensity is $10^2:15^2$, or 100:225, or 1:2.25. In other words, the amount of light falling upon the wall is less than half that falling on the furniture. If we move the light back to 30 feet from the furniture, it would then be 40 feet from the wall and the intensity ratio would be $30^2:40^2$, or 900:1600, or 1:1.78.

The amount of light then falling upon the wall is little better than 4/7 of that falling upon the furniture. We must either use more than one light source, or "paint" with light from a movable source. This implies a static subject, and considerable planning in advance.

In *painting with light,* we employ a constantly moving light, bathing all parts of the subject in the desired volume of light. In addition to the general results of painting with light, we can add subsequently a static light which would "fix" the highlights and produce a definite shadow effect. Naturally, if all parts of the subject were bathed in equal values of illumination, the effect would be dull to say the least. We must *plan* the picture, taking into consideration the desired final effect and managing the problems of additive light values, emphasis of light, and consistent application of light to all parts of the subject.

At first we can discount the possibility of including windows or fixtures, such as chandeliers and table lamps, and concentrate on a simple problem of illuminating a single wall-furniture setup. If we place one light behind the camera, producing a near-axis illumination, we will see that both edges of our field of light appear diminished in brightness. Even if our light did not have "hot-spot" properties, which are overcome only in a few open reflectors or in a broad source of bounce illumination, we will note that the intensity of the illumination is greater at the center of the field than at the edges of the field. Also, the lessening of intensity of the image at the edges of the *picture* field (a lens coverage deficiency) increases this effect. If our wall included in the image is 32 feet wide, and if the light is placed 15 feet away from it, the ratio of illumination from center to edge is about $15^2:22^2$, or about 1:2. The illumination at the edges of the wall space is about 1/2 as intense as at the center. (See diagram, Fig. 29a.) This discrepancy can be overcome by directing the light from its position behind the camera toward each end of the wall for an additional time. It would be difficult to control this exactly; it would involve some mathematics to figure the time and position of the light to obtain an absolutely even illumination. But for all practical purposes we can give an additional 50 per cent exposure at each end, directing the axis of the light to a point about halfway from center to edge and moving the axis of the light to the edge and beyond within 1/2 the duration of the basic exposure, (See Fig. 29b.)

We could, of course, use additional lights, adjusting the field of the second and third lights to compensate for the diminishing-to-edge field of the first light. With a sensitive meter the brightness values of the wall could be balanced in this way. However, the single light has much in its favor and with some careful planning can accomplish astonishing results. A single light at axis position does not create shadows, whether pointed to the center of the field or rotated from side to side. Also, several lights close together "on axis" will not produce shadows in the picture. Reflector floodlamps or spotlights are ideal for this purpose, as they may be used without reflector housing and can therefore be operated close together.

The first experiment in "painting with light" would be to illuminate evenly this 32-foot wall from a parallel plane about 15 feet distant. Suppose that the angle of effective illumination of our reflector would produce at a 15-foot distance a fully illuminated area on the wall about 10 feet in diameter; there would then be three 10-foot circles of illumination on the 32-foot wall from 3 positions of the light on a plane parallel to the wall. Assuming the exposure is 10 seconds for the illuminated areas (with the light fixed in one position), how are we to get a consistent illumination on the entire wall by moving the light across the entire length of the wall from the distance of 15 feet? Referring to Figure 29c, we observe the 3 circles of illumination, their centers, and a hypothetical center beyond the limits of the wall on each side. In order to expose evenly the entire length of the wall with a constantly moving light, we will proceed as follows:

1. Stand at X, opposite B (beyond the edge of the image) and direct the axis of the light to point A (hypothetical point beyond the edge of the wall).

2. Counting seconds, *swing* the light from A to B evenly within 5 seconds; then start to walk with the light so that in another 5 seconds the light is opposite C.

3. Continue to walk with the light so that the light moves across the illumination plane opposite C to D in 10 seconds, from D to E in 10 seconds, and from E to F in 5 seconds. At that point, Y, stop walking and stand with the light outside the image area. Then swing the light from F to G in 5 seconds.

In actuality the light is rotated constantly, not held rigidly directed to the wall. The height of the wall must also be considered; with experience all the detailed problems of timing, even coverage, etc., will be overcome. The above outline may appear complicated at first, but some careful study of the principles involved, and some practice in handling the light, will convince the photographer that "painting with light" is a simple procedure after all!

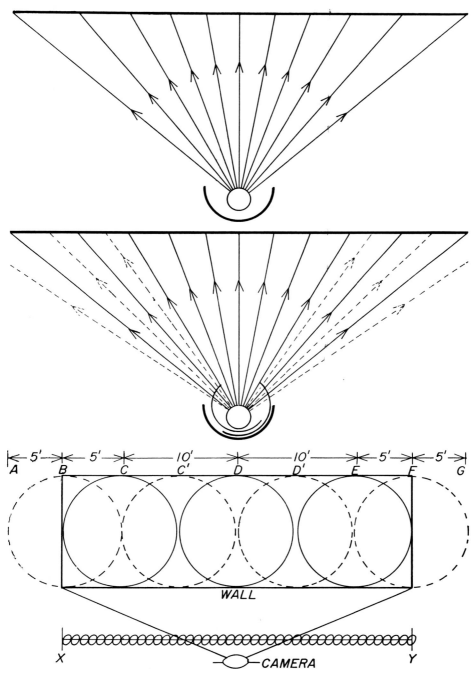

29a. Illumination value diminishes from center of wall opposite light to ends of wall.
29b. Circles of illumination on wall from three positions of the light.
29c. Circles of illumination, and hypothetical continuation beyond wall area.

The Polaroid Land Process offers a marvelous facility for testing the procedures of painting with light. No matter how carefully the problems are anticipated and worked out in advance, a variety of unexpected effects can accrue; unwanted reflections, mergers of tone, etc., can be observed in the Polaroid Land images and avoided in the final exposure.

It is important that the light be kept moving evenly and steadily and that the reflector is not at any time turned toward the lens. The outside of the reflector should be painted a flat black and must not leak light back to the camera; otherwise streaks and flares will show in the image. This is especially important when the light moves within the field of view of the lens. The exposures should be sufficiently long to permit unhurried movement; the photographer carrying the light can move directly in front of the lens (at least 1/3 the distance between lens and subject) without showing in the image—provided he does not *stop* anywhere within the field of view; otherwise his "ghost" image will appear. To repeat: be very careful never to turn the light toward the lens, or even to show the inner edge of the reflector, as this will make a definite streak which will be very hard to retouch in the negative. Do not allow the arm or hand to come within the field of illumination of the light; otherwise they will create an image which will appear as a blurred streak across the field.

A few important points should be discussed before we enter into a detailed description of a more complex problem. It is always advisable first to place the light at various points through which it will be moved during the "painting" process, and to examine the subject from the camera position. This will show any possible bad lighting or reflection effects. Be certain that the camera is *firmly* placed, and that it is never jarred or displaced by operation of the shutter. An easy-fitting lens cap is perhaps the best "shutter" unless one of the self-cocking shutters is used (i. e., a shutter that will open and close, and open and close again on "T" setting without the need for cocking). An assistant is practically a *must* when working with this technique. Check carefully to see that any stationary position of the light used does not show within the field of view. Also check to see that the trailing cord will not show, and guard against its catching on things in the field and displacing them.

The first example of painting with light discussed above was a very simple one, limited only to one general subject-plane (a continuous wall and a few pieces of furniture). There would be no particular problem of depth of illumination; the wall was 15 feet from the light, and if the furniture extended not more than 3 feet from the wall, the nearest object would be 12 feet from the light and would receive about 1.5x the amount of light falling upon the wall. This brightness difference could be compensated for somewhat by pointing the light a bit *upward* (so that the furniture would be generally illuminated more or less by the edges of the field of light). In rotating the light while moving it across the field, give two rotations pointing it upward, and one pointing straight ahead; this would favor a better balance of lighting throughout. Of course, if the same pattern of rotation is not followed throughout there will be obvious differences of values across the image. A metronome provides an ideal means of counting seconds while moving about.

When confronted with a complex subject, such as a large room with groupings of furniture at varying distances from the camera, we *must* make a floor plan in which are shown the relative positions of objects, the planes on which we will carry

30. Hotel St. Francis Cocktail Lounge, San Francisco. This represents an image made chiefly with available light from the Lucite ceiling, plus use of a spotlight to pick out the tufts in the black leather under the bar. The spotlight was carried along by an assistant, following a line roughly parallelling the bar, but well outside the picture area to the right. It was not a continuous movement; the spotlight was operated from a series of "stations," which offered a clear space between the tables, etc., and at each station was swung back and forth in an arc of about 20 degrees. This served to limit the highlights on the tufts in the leather to their proper areas; had the light been applied continuously, the highlights would have been elongated, and there might have been unfortunate accents of light on the chairs. The print was made rather soft to preserve all values in a relative sense, and the engraver increased the effective contrast in the "etching" of the halftone plate. A "display" print would have much more brilliancy than a print for reproduction purposes.

57

the light, and the indicated exposures on each plane. Let us consider a formal room (stylized floor plan shown in Fig. 31). Plane 3 is the wall, Plane 2 the table setups, Plane 1 (nearest the camera) small table and chair setups. Distance from the camera to the center of Plane 1, 18 feet; from the center of 1 to the center of Plane 2, 12 feet; from the center of 2 to the wall (Plane 3), 12 feet; the *light* will pass in front of the camera at a distance of 12 feet from Plane 1. Assuming at first that equal amounts of light are to be given Planes 1, 2, and 3, what will be the increment of light on Planes 2 and 3? The following table will show this in terms of illumination units:

	On Plane 1	*On Plane 2*	*On Plane 3*
Light on 1..............	1	¼	⅑
Light on 2..............	—	1	¼
Light on 3..............	—	—	1
Approx. Totals	1	1¼	1⅜

Assuming that all surfaces throughout have about the same reflectance value, the picture would show a slight increasing brightness in the more distant planes. This is usually to be desired; a decreasing brightness in depth may create a rather "forlorn" mood. However, this ratio may be quite different from the desired brightness key of the picture as a whole, which is determined by visualization. We may wish a literal interpretation of values, or we may wish to stress one of the planes over another, or some particular object within any plane.

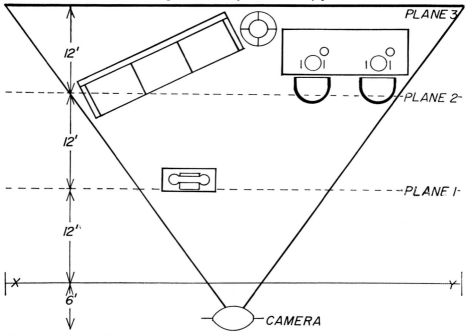

31. Stylized Floor Plan. This is more elaborate and precise than required for a rough sketch for "painting with light," but it shows some of the elements encountered in this process. In a working sketch distances should be accurately noted and position of light fixtures and other objects clearly set down, together with their required specified exposures, etc. It is good to have a multicolored lead pencil, using black for the plan, red for lighting fixtures, green for exposure times, etc.

Remember, illumination units are not *brightness* units (units of exposure). Brightness is a function of reflectance. Before we know just what our final effect is to be, we must evaluate the relative brightnesses of the subject. We may select the wall value as our basic brightness—or any other subject value we choose—or consider a gray card as the basic value and relate all brightnesses to it. If we wish to retain a literal relationship of brightnesses we can base our exposure on the gray card value and by comparison decide where the other brightnesses of the subject will fall on the exposure scale. We will begin by placing the light at 12 feet from the first plane and taking brightness readings of both the gray card and the substances of the furniture, etc. We should list these values, as follows:

I	II	III	IV	V	VI	VII	VIII
	Dark		Chair	*Card*	Table	Lamp	
	wood		fabric		cover	shade*	

Then place the light at 12 feet from the second plane and proceed as above:

I	II	III	IV	V	VI	VII	VIII
Metal		Sofa		*Card*	2nd Lamp		White
table		fabric		Vase	shade*		china
legs							bowls

Then place the light 12 feet from the third plane and proceed as above:

I	II	III	IV	V	VI	VII	VIII
Alcove**		Wood		*Card*	Wall		Window
		trim					***

In the table above, in which we listed various brightnesses in relation to the gray card, we have considered applying the same amount of light to each plane of the subject (with the accumulated brightness-in-depth effect). We have not as yet "visualized" the final print except in terms of literal values, and it will be most helpful here to describe the procedure of photographing this subject literally. No two problems require the same solution.

This table shows the relative brightnesses of the subject only. We should now consider the actual brightnesses (in c/ft^2). Let us assume the brightness of the gray card is 1.6 c/ft^2. With film of Weston tungsten speed of 32, the basic exposure would be about 4 seconds at f/16. As considerable depth of field exists, we will require a small lens stop, and the actual exposure will be about 32 seconds at f/45 (plus reciprocity effect factor).****

---

*Lamp not burning.

**Assuming that the Alcove is of indefinite depth, we will apply a separate light therein after the principal exposure is made. It probably should have a *lighter* value than the wall plane (between VII and VIII).

***Glass windows are most difficult to include because of reflections from the moving light.

****About 2x, in this case. High values will be controlled by proper development. Referring to the first example (single plane), we will consider the length of each plane to be illuminated by the moving light. However, as will be seen in Figure 31, the effective angle of view of the lens results in subject planes of different lengths. But the amount of light directed to each plane *should be the same for every point of the plane.* As the light directed on the near plane and on the second plane will accumulate on the third plane (wall), it is necessary that the entire length of the first and second planes be illuminated so that the third plane will have an equal increment of illumination. Do not attempt to save a little time by illuminating only those parts of the first and second planes within the angle of view of the film; cover the *entire length* of all planes. Lay string, bits of paper, etc., on the floor to define the angle of view of the picture.

59

If our light projects an effective illuminating circle of 8 feet at a distance of 12 feet, and if the distant plane is, say, 32 feet long, we can sketch a diagram such as Figure 32 showing 4 circles of illumination, and the extended circles. Assume the exposure to be 30 seconds at f/45, we will move the light from center-to-center of the circles in 30 seconds, with constant rotation as described above. Our movement plan would be:

1. Stand at X (outside the field of view) opposite B, and direct light from A to B within 15 seconds (constantly rotating).

2. Then, walking, move the light from B to C within 15 seconds.

3. Continuing, move the light from C to D within 30 seconds.

4. Continuing, move the light from D to E within 30 seconds.

5. Continuing, move the light from E to F within 30 seconds.

6. Continuing, move the light from F to G within 15 seconds.

7. Then, standing at Y (outside the field of view) opposite G, direct the light from G to H within 15 seconds.

Move steadily across the field; passing in front of the lens will have no appreciable effect. Proceed with the second and third planes as with the first plane (closing the shutter after each plane is completed). Rehearse by carrying the light across the field several times while counting seconds. The sequence of action can be as follows:

1. Say "open" to an assistant, who removes the lens cap.

2. Start counting, "One-thousand-and-oh, one-thousand-and-oh," until an accurate time-unit rhythm is established. (Watch the second hand of a clock for this.) Or start feeling the rhythm of a metronome. Then on the third "oh," say, the light switch is turned on and counting continues, "One-thousand-and-one, one-thousand-and-two, etc.," while proceeding across the field.

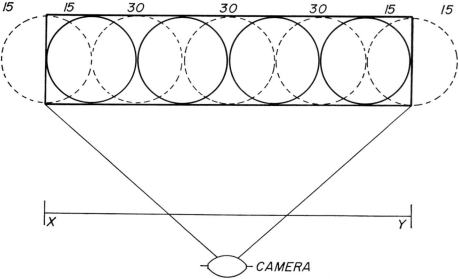

32. This is similar to Figure 29c, except that it relates to the specific description in the text and shows how the dimensions of the subject will indicate the general lighting approach. It is better to keep these descriptions more or less "abstract" because no two problems are alike—yet the basic approach is applicable to all. The photographer must be *inventive!*

3. At the conclusion of travel, turn off the light—and the assistant will immediately cap the lens.

4. General room lights can be turned on, the wires rearranged, etc., and all made ready for "painting" the second plane. Then turn off the room lights and proceed as in (2) above.

5. When the three planes have been "painted," make separate exposures for the alcove, for the external scene through the window, or for the light fixtures and lamps. Also, if any part of the subject needs a special directional light, this can be applied as a separate exposure. The lens is capped between each exposure, of course. It is obvious that the possible range of control by this process of "painting with light" is very great, but everything depends upon precise planning and execution. Architectural and decorative details can be accented by "painting" with a narrow-beam spotlight; dark areas under furniture, in remote areas such as ceiling beams, etc., can be balanced in the same way. With the S.E.I. Meter brightness readings can be taken of small areas under spotlight illumination. In order to avoid the possible strong shadows which will occur when a spotlight is used from any single position (except along the lens axis), the spotlight can be moved about, but always directed in the same area. Sharp highlights can be produced on distant metallic surfaces and forms, but we must be careful not to cast the shadows of these objects on smooth wall and ceiling surfaces.

Our examples have related to plane surfaces—working parallel to the plane of the wall, etc. The problem admittedly does become more complex when we are working with corners, or at an angle to the structural planes. As light-to-subject distance controls exposure (and not lens-to-subject distance), we should plan our "painting" so that the light-to-subject distance is constant in such cases. In other words, instead of painting across the field of view perpendicular to the lens axis, we will have to work with our painting at an angle or curve to the lens axis.

In very high structures, where large expanses of ceiling or vault are included in the image, we will have greater difficulty with the Inverse Square Law effect. We will have to paint these areas with light positioned behind the lens so as to avoid showing the up-tilted light sources in the field of view. Unless the reflector is deep and blackened along the inner edge, it may show in the image when tilted upward to illuminate a high vaulted space. A broad spotlight is advised, and brightness readings can be taken with the S.E.I. Meter from camera position. Compensation in exposure time will be required to balance the inequalities of distance.

Several alternatives to accepting (and then retouching) reflections from glass windows are:

1. Draw the curtains. This automatically implies that the lighting fixtures must be shown as *lighted*. After the principal exposures have been made, turn on the lights and give an additional exposure; open lamps need very short exposure, for otherwise flare may occur. When table lamps are turned on, the brightness of the lamp shades can be placed on Zone VIII or IX, and the exposure adjusted correspondingly. Remember that the shade has received illumination from the traveling light; if it is of light, translucent material it may easily "block up" with too much additional internal exposure. If a feeling of light streaming down from the lamps is required, the exposure must be long enough to record this extra illumination effect as a definitely higher value than the general illumination on areas under the lamp. For instance, if the chair fabric (on Plane 3) is rendered

61

by the general illumination as a Zone IV value, the light falling upon it from the table lamp could be as high as Zone VI or VII.

2. Cover the window glass on the inside with *black* fabric or paper. When all of the sequential exposures have been made, remove the black material, turn off any interior lights, and expose for the external scene as it appears in daylight. In this case, the external scene should be rendered about one Zone higher than the wall brightness. If rendered at the same average value it would appear to be a photomural! (See Fig. 35 for a too-close balance of internal and external brightnesses.) Obviously the external image should not exceed a Zone VII-VIII brightness level (or there will be no feeling of texture and substance); thus in such cases, the wall brightness should not exceed Zone VI-VII value.

3. Remove the glass and cover (outside) with a very dark opaque material. If we cover the window frames and dividing panels with a black material *inside*, they will not pick up light from the interior exposure and may appear unnaturally dark in the photograph. After the sequential exposures, remove the material and expose for the external scene as in (2).

"Painting" is not limited to architectural subjects. The technique is especially valuable in photographing intricate small objects, machinery, etc. The writer once used a small hand torch to illuminate the interior of a complicated electronic instrument, "painting" from behind the camera, emphasizing certain significant areas and minimizing others in terms of brightness variations.

The technique is also valuable in rendering works of art, especially sculpture. In copying paintings *in color*, it will sometimes be found that the intrinsic bright-

33. Interior. This presents a rather complex problem of "painting with light." The principal exposure was made at night; the windows were photographed in the late afternoon preceding the main exposure. Fixtures were turned on after the principal exposure for the proper time (shadows on the beams are from the room lights). Development was in Pyrocatechin.

nesses of the paintings may exceed the effective range of color film; very dark areas cannot be properly exposed without burning up the higher values. In such cases a supplementary spotlight can be directed toward the dark areas from the *same* position as the principal lights (to prevent erratic glare) and, with constant motion, will build up the dark areas to a favorable balance of brightness value. Of course, distortion of values and "hot spots" must be avoided.

It should be stated here that the "intermittency effect"—slight change of reciprocity due to interrupted exposure—will occur with painting procedures as described herein. But with black-and-white material the effect is negligible. With color film a slight over-all increase of exposure is indicated—perhaps a difference of about 1/3 lens stop. (This is in addition to reciprocity effect due to long exposures; tests are indicated in important assignments.) In color photography the potentials of painting with light of mixed colors are tremendously exciting; color compositional effects are practically unlimited.

If the photographer possesses unlimited lighting equipment (à la Hollywood) the painting-with-light procedures are not necessary, since huge floods, reflectors, controlled-area lights, etc., can be used to build up a reasonable illusion of reality. But only a few professionals can boast of such equipment, and it will be found that the painting-with-light technique will give a tremendously flexible controlled illumination.

The reader must recognize that no two situations will be alike and that the foregoing examples only suggest the method. It will be obvious that broad bounce lights can be additionally effective.

34. Interior, Board Room. A good example of "painting with light." The right-hand corner needed a little more light, and the wall shows need of slight additional illumination along the top. The exposure was made at night; the second exposure of the window was made at dawn.

There are many cases where painting with light as described on page 53 is not practical, either in whole or in part. Subjects, such as large industrial plants with complicated installations, may require a tremendous lighting setup (best operated with "slave" flash equipment, especially when figures and machine movements are encountered). For such subjects, what is known as simple "progressive" lighting can be quite satisfactory. This can be accomplished either with flashlamps (concealed from the field of view) or with static light or painting-with-light procedures in specific areas of the subject. In this case each specific area is treated as a separate subject, and there is usually not much effort expended in working out a carefully organized illumination plan for the area as a whole. This technique can be of value in accentuating certain objects and areas in an otherwise semiobscure environment; for example, a picture may be needed in a large printing plant showing the installations of certain equipment. The area may be illuminated to an average low value—say Zone III or IV. The available light in the area may be sufficient for this illumination level, and the specific objects can be photographed by separate exposures and rendered in higher average values—say Zones VI or VII. Control in printing will also serve to emphasize certain areas.

35. Interior. This is a good example of too-close balance of illumination between exterior and interior elements. The illusion is simply one of a curved wall on which a literal photo-mural is mounted. In pictures of this type decisions must be made as to the relative values of "inside" and "outside" areas. Here, if the illumination within had been reduced to about half, the impression of looking *through* the window would have been achieved. Of course the problem of reflections in the glass from the interior lights must not be overlooked; in this case small areas of "bounce" light were applied to ceiling and to walls on either side.

Some workers believe that it is good to refocus for the different planes of the subject as they are illuminated and exposed (both in progressive lighting and painting-with-light procedures). The writer disagrees with this idea for the simple reason that when you alter the focus of the lens you change the size of the image; and even if a foreground subject is not receiving any illumination from a light operating on a more distant and sharply focussed plane, its *silhouette* is smaller than when it was first focussed upon, and the surfaces of the distant subject may slightly overlap the edges of the foreground subject in the completed photograph. It is better to establish an adequate hyperfocal distance and stop the lens down as required to bring all planes into acceptable sharpness. (See Book 1.)

36. Klystron Tube Assembly, Varian Associates, Palo Alto. Made with Hasselblad Camera and 80mm lens. One Heiland Strobe IV light at low level to accent foreground, and second light placed on right at higher level. Shadow behind hand was intentional; it serves to isolate fingers and small part being worked on. Capacitor output was reduced to 50 per cent, and further reduction of effective illumination was achieved by using a polarizer at non-polarizing position to serve as a 2½x neutral density filter. The reduction of light was required because of the small confines of operating space; the close position of the lights produced more illumination (about 5 times as much) than could be used even with the lens stopped to f/22 and allowance made for the extension factor. Diffusing materials could have been placed before the lights to achieve the same result (glass fabric is ideal for this purpose).

65

When working with existing artificial light, it is sometimes impossible to avoid inclusion of light sources (room fixtures or windows) showing in the field of view. As their brightness values will greatly exceed any diffuse brightness of the general subject, we are confronted with an exacting technical problem. If we have the opportunity to plan our exposure, the fixtures can be turned off for a specified time to place them properly on the exposure scale. If we do not have such control over the lights, we can adjust our general exposure for special processes such as the Pyrocatechin Developers or the two-solution formula. If we are working under pressure, with a variety of exposures on one roll of film, for example, we must employ some compensating developer or we shall have hopelessly "burned-up" the flaring images of the light sources.

As described in Books 2 and 4 of this series, a compensating developer is one which gives adequate development to the low and middle densities of the negative and proportionally much less development to the high densities. Water-bath development, two-solution development and "tanning" developers (such as Pyrocatechin) all achieve this objective of high-contrast control. The two-solution development process as outlined on page 8 appears superior to the water-bath process, both in results and ease of application. This two-solution developer controls actual brightnesses up to about Zone XIII (that is, it will allow us to render a Zone XIII placement as a Zone VIII density—opacity—without unduly affecting the low values). It will also partially reduce the flare surrounding the image of a light source. The Pyrocatechin compensating developer definitely "tans" the negative emulsion; that is, it renders it relatively impervious in depth to the developer solution. Practically speaking, only the top layers of the emulsion are developed. Hence, the actual images of the light sources may be revealed with some impression of texture and substance (see Figs. 33a and b, page 108, Book 2). However, the effective film speed is reduced, and due to the color of the developed film (depending somewhat on time of development and the degree of oxidation of the developer) the basic contrast scale of the negative is not always consistent. An example of an interior developed in Pyrocatechin is represented in Figure 33. This picture was made by "painting with light": the principal exposure was made at night; the windows are exposed in late afternoon prior to the main exposure. Fixtures were exposed separately. With ordinary development, low and middle tones would be rendered as usual, but there would be an obvious "blocked-up" quality and flare* in the windows. We should recall that a considerably reduced development time in a normal developer would image the extreme high values quite well, but the low and middle values would be very flat and dull. Special processes such as superproportional reduction and "harmonizing" have their value, but the two-solution process, properly applied, delivers gratifying results.

With an uncoated lens, light sources in the image will probably show a distressing amount of lens flare. Coated lenses minimize this, of course, but we must be on guard against flare from the bellows or other parts of the camera interior. Camera flare gives more trouble than lens flare! The image of a light source may

---

*Flare of this type is due to a scattering of light *within* the depths of the negative emulsion, and to halation from the film base, which exists in small degree even with the nonhalation coating of the back of the negative.

not be included in the field of the negative image, but would fall within the field of view of the lens nevertheless, and would strike the bellows or interior frame of the camera. It then may reflect directly onto the negative with distressing results, or cause indirect reflections which would reduce the general contrast of the image.

When composing a picture of a subject containing light sources in the general field of view, it is wise to explore with the camera from right to left and up and down, just to see if any bright light sources or reflections might fall near the edges of the image. If so, these should be shielded from the lens. A lens hood will help very much in cutting off such extraneous light; but again, the exploration is advised because the ordinary lens hood is circular in form and does not sharply frame the image close to the edges of the negative. The ideal lens hood is rectangular in shape (same proportion as the negative) and positioned before the lens to cut off practically all of the light that does not cover the negative. Actually this "cutting off" cannot be exact because the edge of the lens hood is very much out of focus, and there must be sufficient leeway to avoid any vignetting of the edges of the negative. The efficiency of the before-the-lens lens hood is increased by placing the lens hood opening as far from the lens as possible (on an extended bellows). The "cut-off" of unwanted light will then be much sharper. Of course, the basic position of the lens hood centers on the axis of the lens; when the camera adjustments are used (such as rising or sliding front, tilt front, etc.) the hood *must* be repositioned so as not to "cut off" essential parts of the image. Be very careful to check this—such cut-offs are sometimes difficult to see in the ground glass (especially in the corners), and many a fine negative has been ruined thereby. Cameras which are of fixed design (with no adjustments and using only one lens) sometimes have very effective lens "hoods" built in *behind* the lens, and these, together with efficient baffles within the camera body, serve to cut out most of the extraneous camera flare and give very brilliant images. While lens coating is of undoubted value in increasing brilliancy and reducing flare, we must always remember that the bellows and other parts of the interior of the camera can produce a great amount of scattered light and seriously affect the contrast of the negative. The surface of the negative itself reflects about 30 per cent of the light falling upon it (the gray card reflects 18 per cent); this light is scattered throughout the camera interior, resulting in a certain amount of flare all over the negative during exposure. Through a series of angular baffles and "traps" this internal flare can be minimized, but few, if any, available cameras possess this feature.

Returning to the discussion of light sources in the image, we should recognize the importance of including them when they are definitely part of the subject. Our problem is to control them, not avoid them. There is nothing more distressing than a well-illuminated interior with a "dead" light fixture. Reflections of light sources (from mirrors, highly polished surfaces, etc.) sometimes cause as much trouble as the light sources themselves. Usually many of these reflections can be controlled by Pola-Lights and/or polarizers (see page 77). Of course, such reflections are often of great importance; they represent the surface and substance of materials and seldom should be removed entirely.

Again, surfaces and substances of highly *reflective* quality may be so placed within the subject area that their true appearance is not revealed under the general illumination. We must then *create* the required reflections, usually by directing a spotlight on the surfaces and producing sharp, definite highlights. A good example of this is seen in Figure 30. This picture was made with only the light from the Lucite ceiling (part of which shows in the field) plus "painting" the black leather bar covering with a sharp spotlight. Without this highlight accent, the black leather would appear as a dark and drab material, as it was shielded from the overhead light by the overhang of the bar. Remember, the exposure required to produce images of reflections of the light sources alone is very much less than needed to produce images of a diffuse surface. When "painting" with a spotlight, we should usually rotate the light while carrying it across the field; otherwise the highlights might take on the appearance of a thin line, giving a false impression of form. In Figure 30, the spotlight was operated from several "stations."

Glass and Other Transparent and Translucent Objects

With subject matter of this description, the impression of light and substance is of greatest importance. With glass, the feeling of *transparency* must be preserved. Form is indicated in terms of "edge" and highlight. "Edge" must be shown as dark against light background, or light against dark background. Highlights must relate to the form of the object. Obviously, painting with light or the use of broad reflectant light sources might produce false highlights—that is, highlights which would not clearly define the form or which would distort it. Backlighting, top or base lighting, subtle lighting for highlights, background control, etc., must all be adjusted for the particular problem at hand. There are no formulas which will satisfy all requirements. Reference is made to the excellent glass photographs used in the Steuben Glass Company advertising. While sometimes overdramatized for advertising impact, these pictures usually convey an astonishingly fine impression of the substance and form of the subjects.

Many industrial subjects, which include test tubes and retorts, suffer because of too great complexity of lighting and attendant reflections and highlights. A good rule of thumb is to use as few lights as possible, adding lights only when absolutely necessary. Much of the visual impression of glassware is associated with *environment;* the mood of brilliancy, smoothness and sparkle can be depreciated by a drab, unrelated environment. The procedure is one of careful appraisal of the effects of light, and gradual addition of light until the subject is revealed in the simplest and most intense aspect. Work first for the delineation of form through sharp edges and broad highlights; then add the "sparkle" by using a small, sharp spotlight (usually from above or below the subject and at a considerable distance), with care not to cast shadows or create complex internal reflections.

Translucent objects present their own particular problems. A translucent object shows both transmitted light and diffuse surface reflections—together with sharp highlights (depending on the nature of the substance). Obviously, the subtle variations of brightness must be preserved in the image; a blank chalk-like impression thoroughly defeats the interpretive object. Mere contrast will not achieve the impression of translucent brilliancy. Again, the lighting should be simple, gradually assembled in relation to the acceptable visual impression. Too much backlighting will perhaps exaggerate the transparency; too much surface lighting will minimize it. Sharp highlights will perhaps be best applied in a separate exposure, as their formal effects can be seen more clearly. Viewing the subject through a Wratten No. 90 Viewing Filter will accentuate the impression of form—or lack of it—as defined by the highlights.

A complete exposition of the photography of subjects such as glass, plastics, etc., is beyond the scope of this book. We are concerned with fundamentals of procedure and technical concept here; the photographer must carry on into the realms of specialization. Nevertheless it is not out of place here to suggest that the photographer observe and study both good and bad examples of applied photography and preserve examples in his files. In studying pictures other than his own he should attempt to visualize the subject and also the lighting techniques used. Then he will be in a position to think about what *he* would have done in interpreting the subject. Would he alter the basic brightness range? Are the highlights sufficiently sharp? Are there too many light sources used? Are the reflections from existing lights disturbing, or do they create an impression of realism, etc.?

37. Glass Medallion, photo by Jacques Schnier (courtesy Grattan English, designer). This object, mounted at the base of a window, is designed to be seen by transmitted light. It is a deeply etched and sand-blasted glass of considerable thickness. This picture was made with a strong spotlight placed out of doors and directed at the appropriate angle to the medallion. A second diffuse light within provides a balance of illumination. In this print no attempt has been made to equalize the values from one side of the medallion to the other; due to restricted space out of doors, the spotlight could not be placed at a distance which would have overcome the inverse-square effect. In such cases, "dodging and burning" of the print is justifiably required.

69

38. Transistor Assembly. Made with Hasselblad Camera and 80mm lens with extension tube. The principal light is from the microscope illuminator (low-power microscopes are used in this exacting work), and the general diffuse light comes from the fluorescent lighting of the laboratory. The microscope light strikes the main subject at an angle and creates an area of bright light on the white table covering. This could have been "printed down" in the print to emphasize the main subject. The brightness values were read with the S.E.I. Meter and proper compensation made for lens extension. Fortunately, the balance of light was such that normal development of the negative was indicated; had the environmental light been of lower intensity, "bounce" light would have been introduced and/or Normal-minus development given the negative. The exposure was just right for the principal subject; more exposure would have been modified—not the light on the main subject—had the balance been wrong.

The long-practiced methods of controlling glare and reflections from silver-ware, polished metal, jewelry and like materials, by placing the objects in a "tent" of light-diffusing fabric or applying putty or powder, etc., are now rather obsolete. The introduction of polarizing devices has opened a large field of reflection control —especially with the Kodak Pola-Lights used with a conventional polarizer on the lens (see page 77). However, "tents" and enclosures of diffusing and reflecting materials have their uses, especially when "highlight" light is also used. Light can be applied to a static subject by using a moving reflector of the diffusing type, applying light to all parts of the subject during exposure. This is somewhat related in technique and effect to painting with light (page 53). In all cases where "static" subjects are involved, we can make our exposures separately for each type of lighting employed (using extreme care not to displace or jar the camera or subject in any way). The accumulation of brightness values can be measured and charted on the Exposure Record.

A typical example would be as follows: The subject is an intricate bronze statue, with a generally dark "ground" tone and sharp highlights. If the statue were photographed entirely by diffused light, the highlights would be far too broad and the character of the substance inaccurately rendered. Visualizing the image of a bronze statue, we could think of the ground tone (the basic tone of the metal under diffuse illlumination) as about Zone IV value. The highlights, if sharp, would be above Zone VIII. If the entire figure is to be illuminated from one broad source of diffuse light, the procedure is simple: merely measure the brightness value of the relatively flat surfaces and place them on Zone IV of the exposure scale. If the figure is to be illuminated by a moving diffuse light, place the light at the distance at which it is to be used and take the brightness reading on an area of the subject showing maximum diffuse reflectance. (Refer to the technique of paint-ing with light, page 77, where evaluation of a continuously moving source of illumination is described.) After the exposure is made, apply a direct light for the chief purpose of producing highlights. As the highlights are the direct reflection of the light source, their brightness value is far greater than the diffuse reflections produced. With this placement the highlights should be sufficiently above Zone VIII to appear quite sharp and bright. No matter how bright they are, they must have a certain "broadness"; otherwise they will not produce a visually adequate effect. Either the direct light must be sufficiently broad to produce the desired effect, or it must be moved through an arc so as to provide an effectively broad light source. Do not move the light in a circle only, or a single direction; if you do, the highlights might take on an obvious "form." Rather, move the direct light in a highly irregular pattern, covering a space about 1 or 2 feet square at a distance of about 8 to 12 feet from the subject. The necessary highlight quality can be appraised visually before the exposure is made. One advantage of the moving light is that it would minimize the shadow edges that might show on the relatively flat surfaces of the subject. Of course, if the direct light is moved too much the highlights will be distorted, and the space and substance of the figure distorted as well. As all subjects present their peculiar problems, the example given here is to be considered only as suggestive of actual procedure—not to represent any one situation. A typical entry in the Exposure Record might be:

Zones	I	II	III	IV	V	VI	VII	VIII	IX	X
Exposure Units	1	2	4	8	16	32	64	128	256	512

Placement of diffuse
   illumination from   (8)
   diffuse light   x

Placement of diffuse
   illumination from   (2)
   direct light   x

Placement of highlights from direct light: x.............up

The accumulation of exposure units for the diffuse brightnesses from both diffuse and direct light (total of 10 units) would fall a little above the original placement. If there is any doubt that the density of the highlights will be sufficient, normal-plus-development can be given the negative. As the diffuse-brightness areas are relatively low on the exposure scale, additional development will not have much effect on them. Also, a certain control in printing is feasible to adjust for any imbalance in the relative values of the subject.

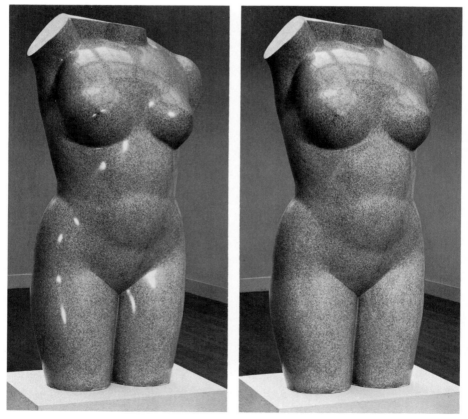

39. Torso, by B. Bufano. This figure was illuminated both by museum skylight and tungsten lights behind sheets of Polaroid. The polarizer on the lens was first adjusted so as *not* to reduce the skylight reflections; then the Polaroid was rotated so the direct reflections from the tungsten light were eliminated, but the diffuse light therefrom was retained.

Control of Background Values

In photographing small objects for which light, shadowless backgrounds are required, a setup as sketched in Figure 40 is most helpful. Briefly, it is a table composed of a top sheet of glass on which the object is supported. About 2 feet below is a sheet of opal glass, or a sheet of ordinary glass covered with architect's tracing cloth which serves as the translucent background. Under this is a bank of fluorescent lights (or a close group of tungsten lights). A simpler plan would be to have as the background, in place of the opal glass, a smooth white card of plastic or fabric on which light from a diffused source is directed from above and to the sides, but *shielded* from the surface of the top glass. The background must be suffused with *even illumination*. A second sheet of glass can be installed (as per Fig. 40) on which objects, shields, etc., can be placed for special effects.

The objects are photographed with any desired illumination—single or multiple lighting—completely independent of background effect. Of course, if the background is opal glass or a white card, there is certain to be some "pick-up" of brightness and possibly some broad shadow effects. These would usually be absorbed in the subsequent exposure for a white background, but if they appear troublesome the background should be covered with a black card or fabric during the exposure of the objects lying on the top glass.

The objects are exposed to render them with the desired values and contrasts. Pola-Lights and polarizers can be used to control reflections (see page 77). Sharp spotlights can be used to produce brilliant highlights. The objects will cast no visible edge shadow, as they are placed on a sheet of clear glass well above the background plane. After the first exposure is made, the black card or fabric is removed from the background plane and the white surface illuminated with a smooth diffuse light (by transmission or reflection). The intensity of the illuminant is not important except that it should be sufficiently high to give the desired back-

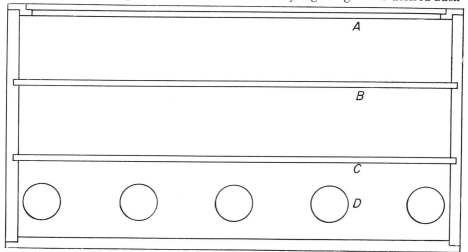

40. Diagram of Shadowless-Background Apparatus (not necessarily to scale).
"A" Clear glass, safety plate preferred.
"B" Opal glass; serves as shelf for background material with incident light.
"C" Opal glass, for primary diffusion.
"D" Fluorescent or "Lumiline" incandescents (caution with Lumiline: heat!).

73

ground brightness without unduly long exposure time. A "spill" of light into the room, or a pick-up from some bright environmental object, might affect the values of the object being photographed, especially if it was of high reflectance.

The brightness reading of the background is placed on the appropriate zone of the exposure scale. With the subject lights off, make a second exposure for the background alone. Be especially careful not to displace or jar the camera or subject between exposures. The background should appear in the image as a continuous tone of the desired Zone—Zones VI, VII, VIII or IX, as the case may be—and the object will appear against this background with a well-defined edge and without shadows. Figs. 41a and b show the same subject photographed against a close white background and a shadowless background. Shadows in (a) are disturbing.

Determination of the proper background value will depend on the actual brightness values of the objects photographed (especially their edge brightness). Also, we must watch for edge reflections on the subject *from the background*. The subject must be carefully examined with the background light on; such edge reflections might be controlled by use of the polarizer, which should then be used when the background exposure is made. In this case it is advisable to have the polarizer on the lens from the start, set at a non-polarizing angle (or to any angle desired). The position to control reflections *from the background* should be determined before the first exposure is made. After the first exposure, rotate the polarizer to the desired position and expose for the background. This will prevent any possible disturbance of camera position. Do not neglect to apply the proper exposure factor (2½x) for *both* exposures.

Obviously it would be possible to balance the illumination on both object and background for the desired effect in a single exposure. But the divided-exposure procedure is much simpler and gives a wide range of possible effects without having to alter the relative intensities of the lights. Background values can vary over the field as required by adjustment of lights, or use of translucent materials over them. Such effects should be examined from the direction of the lens to be certain of their position and values in the field of view.

41. Gears and Spring. (a) represents the effect of photographing small objects against a very close white background; the shadows destroy the integrity of edge and form. In (b) the shadowless background serves to define the forms clearly.

Frequently it is desired to photograph a light object against a white background. In such cases shadows sometimes can be used to good effect to clarify form. On the other hand, the technique described above can be used to advantage with the following modification: after the first exposure of the subject is made, *advance the lens* (thereby creating a larger, but out-of-focus, image of the subject on the focal plane). Then proceed to make the background exposure for Zone VIII or IX placement. The effect will be as follows: the light object will appear against the white background, but separated by a "halo" of darker value. The greater distance the lens is advanced, the broader this halo (and the more diffuse). The outer edge of the halo can be sharpened by stopping down the lens. But the basic size of the halo will depend upon the distance of the lens from the focal plane. (See Figs. 42a and b.) Any object longer than its width may produce an unwanted effect with this procedure unless a lens of very long focal length is used. The width of the halo is greater the farther it is from the center of the field.

We must not overlook the fact that any white background will add a certain amount of general flare to the entire image, and the low values of the subject will be affected. Lower placement of the shadow values than normally indicated—or longer development time—is required to render the desired contrast (that is, the contrast which would result if the subject were photographed against a dark or middle-gray background).

A typical Exposure Record entry of a controlled background exposure would be:

Zones	I	II	III	IV	V	VI	VII	VIII	IX	X
Subject		x							x	
Background									x	

Other possible controls would include background illumination of varying brightness for special effect: for example, covering a brightness range of Zone VI to Zone IX *across* the field. This would require careful adjustment of the lights,

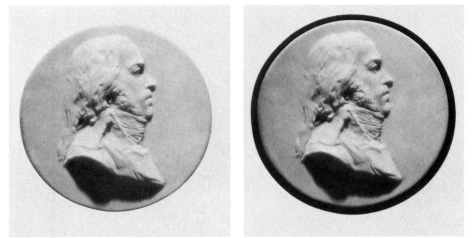

42a and b. Unglazed French Porcelain Plaque (courtesy, California Palace of the Legion of Honor, San Francisco). This subject is extremely flat and unglazed, reflecting only diffuse light. Sharp sidelighting was given to accent the low relief. In (a) the round form is rather vague against the light background; in (b) the dark circular field (produced by advancing the lens for the background exposure) isolates the plaque from the light background.

75

and the values well worked out in advance on the exposure chart. Interesting combination images could be produced by successive images of objects on different planes—from the top glass to the background. As these effects are impossible to see all at one time on the ground glass, the forms should be sketched on the glass itself as they are composed; in that way we know what the relative compositional effects would be.

43. Botanical Photograph, by Pirkle Jones, San Francisco. This is a good example of the shadowless-background technique. The delicate tendrils of the vine are clearly rendered without confusing shadows or flare. The light on the vine itself was mostly environmental, and a certain amount of translucence is observed in the leaves. Only rarely in nature can ideal background conditions of this kind be found; the sky may serve as a soft "shadowless background," but the subjects seldom can be suitably arranged in relation to it. Subjects such as this, hanging in space in front of smooth backgrounds, are difficult to keep motionless; placement on the top glass of the shadowless-background apparatus serves to prevent movement.

Obviously, this technique has interesting applications in color photography; shadowless backgrounds of any color or brightness can be obtained by use of colored lights or cards, etc.

If considerable work of this character is to be done, a fixed or portable apparatus can be designed in which the glass, background and lights will be conveniently placed and controlled. For occasional work the top glass can be supported by two chairs or boxes, using a sheet or large card, for the white background. Ordinary reflector floodlamps are excellent for the background illumination. *Shield the lens and the subject from the background lights!*

Several important points should be stressed.

A. Arrange the subject on the glass from the viewpoint of the lens.

B. Be certain the angle of view of the lens will not include the edges of the background area; hence the need for a fairly large "stage" and/or a lens of fairly long focal length.

Photography with Polarized Light

In natural light we frequently use a polarizer before the lens to deepen the blue sky (maximum effect at 90° angle to the sun) and to remove or minimize reflections from glass, polished wood, etc., at about 35° angle to the plane of the subject. The effects are observed visually and are therefore quite dependable. The polarizer can be used with great advantage on subjects illuminated by artificial light, and the same angle of maximum effectiveness (35°) holds as with natural light. However, with the polarizer alone we are always limited to exposing at the polarizing angle; we cannot photograph objects "head-on" and control unwanted reflections. The control of reflectant surfaces is greatly expanded by polarizing the light and also using a polarizer on the lens. The Kodak Pola-Light is a very practical piece of equipment and is worthy of much study and experimentation. Two Pola-Lights are usually used for adequate balance. With these lights and the polarizer on the lens, paintings may be photographed without the annoying varnish sheen; rough, highly reflectant surfaces can be "cleared" and the basic textures revealed to an astonishing degree; and some metallic surfaces can be reduced to an almost "earthy" quality. Obviously, it would be simple to distort the impression of substance to a profound degree, and the visual appraisal of the combined polarizing effect should be most carefully made from the *position of the lens*. The polarizing screens before the lights can be turned to any angle; usually a vertical position of the axis (indicated by an arrow indented on the pola-screen) is "normal." If two or more Pola-Lights are used, the screens must all be at the same polarizing position. Then the polarizer before the lens is rotated until the desired effect is obtained. As the effects may be determined by visual examination, there is no need to elaborate further here except to repeat the fact that reflections are important parts of the shapes and images of substances, and if we thoughtlessly remove reflections we may create distortion instead of conviction.

The exposure increase with the polarizer before the lens is about 2½x. This indicates that it would require 2½x the normal exposure to render an *unpolarized* surface with the same density on the films as it would appear without the polarizer. The polarizing effect is one of reducing the brightnesses of areas subject to polarization; we *can* determine the amount of additional exposure required to render them in normal density, but there is little purpose in this, as we desire to *produce* the polarizing effect and there would be no sense in overcoming it by additional

44. Flowers in a Vase, by Henri Fantin-Latour (1836-1904), courtesy, California Palace of the Legion of Honor, San Francisco. This is a combined image; the left portion shows glare from the illumination (Pola-Lights) without the polarizer in effective position before the lens. The right portion shows the elimination of glare by properly positioning the polarizer in relation to the position of the Polaroid discs before the lights. In the right-hand portion, one can see all of the values of color and detail, the brush strokes and the texture of the canvass. It will be obvious that a meter reading of the painting *with* the glare would give too high a figure; hence the brightness reading should be made through the polarizer in optimum position.

exposure. As the effect of the polarizer can be determined visually, we need only remember to increase the exposure $2\frac{1}{2}$x when the polarizer is used.

With the Pola-Light and the polarizer before the lens, the problem of exposure determination is not so simple. With the lights alone we can measure the relative brightnesses. But with the polarizer on the lens, an exaggerated effect obtains; the exposure increase over normal illumination sometimes will be as high as 40x.

The procedure can be as follows:

1. Set up a subject under normal lights, placed for maximum compositional and formal effects.

2. Examine with *polarizer*. If reflections are too dominant:

3. Set up *Pola-Lights* and adjust the screens to their "normal" position. Then:

4. Examine with *polarizer* and determine the most effective position therefor.

5. Measure brightnesses with or without polarizer, as required, and determine exposure.

For color photography certain filters are designated for use with the Pola-Lights to compensate for the transmission effects of the polarizing screens. The early Kodak Pola-Screen gave a light-balancing effect similar to an 81 light-balancing filter (late-model Pola-Screens are more neutral in value), but when the Pola-Lights are used a further color effect is noted (in addition to any reciprocity effect from long exposure).

In black-and-white photography, standard color filters can be used in conjunction with the polarizer and the Pola-Light; be certain to apply the filter exposure factor as well as the polarizer exposure factor. For example, the use of a Wratten K2 Filter with tungsten light will require 1.5x exposure. With a polarizer combined with the filter, the exposure would be $Ex1.5x2\frac{1}{2}$ = about 4x. With polarizer, filter and Pola-Light screen, the exposure factor might be $1.5x2\frac{1}{2}x4$ about 16x. Surface qualities affect the total factor.

A copy of a painting with and without Pola-Lights is shown in Figure 44.

To repeat: the effects of color filters are anticipated by experience and knowledge of their action in modifying the monochromatic values of subject colors. The effects of the polarizers and the Pola-Lights may be appreciated before exposure. With the Pola-Lights and the polarizer on the lens, the effects should be determined visually by viewing through the polarizer; the exposure can be determined by measuring the brightnesses through the polarizer set at the working angle. Exposure factors relate to non-polarizing surfaces; naturally, as the polarizing effect appears, the polarized areas are deepened in value.

The following table will serve to clarify the above-mentioned statements, and is based on an actual test. A gray card was placed before the lens and the lights were directed upon it at an angle of $45°$ (no glare obtained; the card reflected only diffuse light). The table gives brightness values and exposure factors:

Pola-lights:	→	Polarizer: None	20 c/ft²	—
Pola-lights:	→	Polarizer: →	8 c/ft²	2.5x
Pola-lights:	→	Polarizer: ↗	5 c/ft²	4x
Pola-lights:	→	Polarizer: ↑	3 c/ft²	6.5x

If the card possessed any *glare*, the last two exposure factors would have been considerably increased. The arrows show, of course, the axis of the polaroid before the lights and the polarizer before the lens. Readings were made through the polarizer with the S. E. I. Meter.

Sometimes "pockets" of deep shadow, or unruly reflective surfaces, make direct lighting or highly diffused "bounce" lighting unsatisfactory. In such cases it may be that a broadly diffused axis light of relatively low intensity is indicated. As such light is practically shadowless, highlight will be rather broad; due to a possible reciprocity effect because of very low intensity, we may find it necessary to place the "fill-in" brightness on a higher Zone (III instead of II, for example).

In photographing black objects such as a telephone, a typewriter or dark pottery, or intricate brilliant objects such as jewelry, small and complex machinery, etc., the basic exposure should be based on this broadly diffused axis light; then a sharply directional light can be discreetly applied to produce sparkling highlights. If the light source is directed to the ceiling or wall or some suitable large reflecting surface, the subject will be bathed with light. This light should define the basic exposure (with full consideration for possible reciprocity effect). Obviously, the use of a sensitive light meter is necessary for full control of exposure under such conditions. Refer to the section on bounce light, page 43.

When using low values of diffuse light, it is frequently difficult, if not impossible, to take a direct reading of the subject except with extremely sensitive meters, such as the S.E.I. A reading can be taken from the white side of the Kodak Neutral Test Card (90 per cent reflectance) and its value placed between Zones VII and VIII of the exposure scale, thereby assuring approximate related placements for the lower brightnesses of the subject on the exposure scale. (This assumes that all surfaces considered are equally illuminated.) If the light is sufficiently strong, the reading from the gray card (18 per cent reflectance) can be taken and this value placed on Zone V of the exposure scale.

If the light source is too faint for adequate brightness readings from the gray card, the card can be brought closer to the light (to a distance related by 1/2, 1/3 or 1/4 to the subject distance and the resulting meter values modified by the inverse square ratio factor. For example, if the card were brought to 5 feet from the light source (a window or light fixture) and an exposure of 1 second for a Zone V placement was indicated, at a distance of 20 feet from the window an exposure of 16 seconds (4^2) would be in order. In addition, after this mathematical exposure relationship was established, there would be a further increase for reciprocity effect; in this case perhaps 2 or 3 times (see page 4). The reciprocity effect varies with different types of film.

When the S.E.I. meter is used, light values as low as 1/300 (0.03) c/ft^2 can be accurately measured; lower values can be determined by using the gray card methods described previously. However, when such low brightness values are employed, the resulting exposure-reciprocity effect may be extreme, and the exposures impractically long.

45. Technical Lecture. Made with Hasselblad Super-Wide Camera and its 38mm Zeiss Biogon. This picture simulates an actual daily situation; but because of the flat fluorescent lighting of the classroom, a lighting composition had to be devised that would be both expressive and logical in relation to actuality. The computer device was brought closer to the lectern than it would usually be placed. An extreme "near-far" approach was employed; the components of these machines are usually quite small and do not "read" well except at close range. The speaker was illuminated from a soft spotlight placed on the left. The computer was lighted from another spot source placed on the right. The lens was carefully shielded from both lights. A strong "bounce" light was directed to the ceiling to enforce the existing illumination. Certain improvements could be made in printing this picture as it appears here: the grid top of the computer could be considerably deepened in tone to better "separate" it from the audience, and the hand of the speaker could be "printed down" a bit. People who are not models in the professional sense become impatient and fatigued, and pictures of this type are usually made under considerable pressure of time. Advance "setups" should be worked out whenever possible.

81

46. Erich Leinsdorf, Conductor. Made with Hasselblad Camera and 250mm lens. One Heiland Strobe IV light placed high on the right and a little behind the subject; second light placed at 3x the distance of the first light, positioned fairly high and to the *right* of the camera. "Finding" lights were used to compose and establish desired balance of illumination. From a strictly technical viewpoint we might desire more textural rendition in the shadowed areas. Here is where "seeing" (visualization) can indicate the desired "departure-from-reality." In this case raising the shadows one Zone in value would have weakened the dramatic impact of the image. The reasons for creative decisions are found *in the pictures themselves*, not in any theory of technique or intellectual patterns of thought. Creativity implies command both of vision and the means to express it. Conventionally speaking, this image could stand some retouching; skin textures, lines under the eyes, etc. In the original print these appear logically expressive.

PORTRAITURE

I am in complete disagreement with those who believe in rigid plans of illumination in portrait photography (or in any other type of photography, for that matter). Lighting formulas inhibit expressive interpretation. Each and every face presents a specific problem for the photographer; not only of physical form, line and texture, but of expressive and interpretive qualities as well. Visualization is primarily concerned with the final picture—not only with the technical aspects of making the photograph.

In the attempt to set forth a basic approach to technique, I may sometimes give the impression that artificial lighting is valid only if it reproduces the effects of natural lighting. I have no intention of supporting this idea, for the simple reason that artificial lighting is more than just illumination; it is an instrument of control, and tremendous "departures from reality" are possible through its uses. In order to express these basic facts properly, we must have some simple points of *realism* on which to establish our methods and conduct our experiments. Once we can evaluate the properties of illumination and command their use, we are in a position to express ourselves freely, without dependence upon arbitrary rules and regulations.

Therefore, I believe it is logical to base this discussion of portrait lighting on the several general types of lighting described on page 90 and those following. There are, of course, certain specific problems peculiar to the subject of portraiture, but in general, lighting for portrait photography involves no esoteric procedures.

For practical reasons we should do a lot of experimenting with lighting on heads and figures without actually exposing negatives. This "dry shooting" will economically add to our experience in managing lights. Select as a model any available person. Study the forms and textures of the face, and the relationship of the physical aspects to the subject's character as you know it. Place one light (the future "main" light) near the lens axis, then move it in an arc and at various heights so that the angle of illumination on the face is constantly sharpened. You will undoubtedly find that at one rather definite angle of illumination the physical and expressive qualities of the face will be most acutely revealed; suddenly the "meaning" of line and contour is asserted in relation to the particular problem. It is obvious that not only the horizontal position of the light, but usually (and most important) the vertical position must be considered. And, needless to say, the camera angle to the subject is of great importance too, both in horizontal and vertical positions.

Once we have more or less decided upon the most effective position of the main light with regard to the maximum revelation of the subject's sculptural and expressive qualities, we can then experiment with appropriate brightness balance and tonal values. Remember, the use of a fill-in light is *not* mandatory; perhaps the subject will demand a strong, mask-like interpretation with firm, harsh shadows; on the other hand, a generous amount of fill-in may be necessary. Each problem must be solved in its own way. See Figure 2, page xii.

When the lighting which provides the desired visual effect is achieved, we should then make careful brightness readings. It is here that visualization of the final print is so important; merely balancing the lighting to the satisfaction of the eye does not imply that the final print will present the effect desired. When the brightness readings are made and entered on the exposure record, we can see at a glance whether it would be simpler to give more or less development in relation to the indicated exposure, or to rely on normal development and adjust the brightness of the subject by manipulation of the distance and/or intensity of the lights. This statement should be given much thought; it is basic to the whole principle of visualization and control. The procedure is: adjust the lighting for satisfactory visual effects; visualize the print accordingly; then analyze brightnesses, and adjust illumination balance and exposure placement to achieve desired results.

As increasing numbers of lights are used, the eye impression becomes less accurate, and the need for careful brightness readings more important. Remember this: the satisfying eye impression relates to the visualization of the final print, but to achieve the visualized image, the procedures of exposure and development depend upon positive knowledge of the brightnesses and brightness-range of the subject; we cannot fully trust the eye!

If we wish to illuminate eye sockets, we will usually employ axis light or a sufficiently intense general environmental light in addition to the main light and the other lights used. As a rule, it will not be found feasible to use even a strong secondary light to illuminate eye sockets; complex and unpleasant shadow effects may result. It is important to recognize that the amount of light required to produce catchlights in the eye will be much less than that required to place skin on Zone II; the catchlight is a reflection of the light source. Hence a relatively weak light will produce catchlights without changing the brightnesses of any part of the subject to any appreciable extent. A 25-watt lamp at 10 feet from the subject without reflector will create a sharp catchlight without producing any exposure effect when general illumination of average intensity is employed.

Frequently the axis light is used as the principal secondary light. While this produces a falling off of brightness of planes at a sharp angle to the lens axis and of planes behind the main subject plane, it does gives a good general illumination and supplies eye-socket illumination. It is best to use a diffused light source for the axis light when employed in this way; strong secondary highlights might be very disturbing.

If the axis light were at the exact center of the lens, or if it surrounded the lens (a circular tube light), no shadows would appear. But with the light only a few inches off the lens center we will find definite small shadows; if these are sharp they may be very unpleasant. Hence, using as broad a light source as possible will minimize this shadow effect. Of course, with a too broad light source the catchlights in the eyes will be too wide, giving the eyes a "glazed" effect, and the secondary highlights on the features may be too broad. Only by trial can we arrive at a personally satisfactory combination.

With certain subjects we may wish to use only a strong main and/or top light, and rely on general diffuse environmental light to support the shadowed parts of the subject (or we can use a diffuse reflected light). Top and general diffuse lighting is favorable for elderly women; on the other hand, perhaps we will have an elderly subject for which a strong sculptural lighting is imperative. This is mentioned just as a reiteration that we must not follow arbitrary formulas; we must always *explore*.

An effect produced by strong crosslighting, sometimes called the "core" effect, can be used for dramatic purpose and is quite justified in powerful lighting com-

47. Dr. Howard Hanson at Audition (Eastman School of Music, Rochester, N. Y.) Made with Hasselblad Camera, 135mm lens. Main light on head from left; very strong light on figure of violinist reflected in Dr. Hanson's glasses. Shadow on left side of head illuminated by reflection from strong light on violinist. The light on the violinist was about 8 times as intense as the main light on the head, to maintain sufficient brightness of the reflected image. This photograph simulates an actual observed situation under normal lighting conditions—but the normal illumination was about 100 times less intense than that required to make this photograph. With a very large aperture and fast film, it might be approached with "available" light.

positions. The "core" can be completely black or brought to any desired value by use of the axis or environmental light (Fig. 50, page 92).

It may be trite to say, "Use the fewest possible lights"; the approach should be, "Use lighting most efficiently for the desired expressive results." Everyone has seen examples of grossly overlighted portraits; the multiple catchlights, the forced use of spotlights and reflectors, etc. One tries to conjure up the expressive authenticity of such lighting—and usually without success! Again, we are familiar with the extremely competent style of portraiture wherein every subject is meticulously lighted, exposed, printed and presented—and where every subject looks like every other subject. The domination of formula assures an average level of mood, and one seeks in vain to discover the thrilling *presence* of the individual.

Exotic portraiture relates more to applications of lighting than to any hocus-pocus of equipment or techniques. In other words, *method* and *effect* are often confused. The routine lighting formulas include a wide range of applications, from a single light to a complex Christmas tree of lamps, reflecting screens and other impedimenta of the profession. As film speeds increase we will find more opportunity in simple lighting effects, approaching the feeling and quality of normal "available" light.

Environmental Portraiture

Environment plays an important part in the expressive portrait image. A background is not just something against which something else is placed; it should be an integral part of the total concept and expression. It can suggest space, it can suggest the personal accessories of the subject, it can be a definite *construction* of light, shade, forms and movements to accent the characteristics of the subject and create or intensify moods. Naturally, the background values must be evaluated along with the brightnesses of the principal subject; the eye cannot be trusted to perceive all possible mergers of tone. The values should be charted on the Exposure Record sheet, and checked and double-checked to assure the proper brightness separations. These small mergers, so difficult for the eye to grasp when viewing the whole, may be very distressing in the final print.

The "environmental portrait" involves more than just background control. It relates to the philosophy of "seeing" and interpretation. It is not necessarily concerned with obvious relationships—such as a literary man pictured in his library, or a mathematician before his blackboard. It reaches farther into the personality of the individual portrayed, associating him with elements suggestive of his inner qualities. Examples are legion: I think of the portrait of Edna St. Vincent Millay by Arnold Genthe—the fragile and spiritual poet in an environment of spring blossoms; not cut flowers in a studio, but the budding branches of an orchard tree on a moody day. And Stieglitz' portrait of the figure of O'Keefe standing by a gate, suffused in a glowing translucent light. And Edward Weston's color portrait of Dody Warren Weston, a partial figure against a flaming paint-spattered wall. These associations are magical, they can be described only by the photographs themselves, and they suggest new worlds of interpretation. The examples cited above were all made in natural light, but controlled artificial light would further extend the possibilities of this approach. Unfortunately, many otherwise splendid portraits reflect the mood of the studio and not the mood of environmental actuality or environmental symbolism.

48. Eldridge T. Spencer, F.A.I.A., Stanford University. Made with Hasselblad Camera and 80mm lens. One light on right not far from lens axis. Second light on far left to illuminate upper corner of wall model of the university. Third light bounced from walls behind and to left of camera. Foreground table "printed down" a little to accentuate white ruler in hand. This can be considered an environmental portrait, and conveys both the personality of the subject and an impression of the institution which he serves as Chief of Planning.

Environmental portraiture is one of the most rewarding aspects of photography. It provides opportunity for highly imaginative organizations of individuals and symbolic environments and accessories. As mentioned in the text, the subject does not have to be photographed with *obvious* associations of home, business, or profession. He can be integrated into a symbolic composition which creates mood and perceptive impulse. In professional advertising and journalistic work this approach is increasing in favor; witness, for example, the magnificent photographs by Arnold Newman made for *The New York Times* advertisements.

In search of symbolic environment we might place a highly intellectual person in a composition of precise instrument dials, gleaming with glass and chrome and cryptic symbols. The impression of precision, sharpness and complexity might very well relate to the personality of the subject. Please note that such a picture is not expressing the trite relationship between his specific profession and the "background" (such as might be the case were he an electronic engineer or machinist). True environmental portraiture involves the association of moods, symbols and oblique relationships rather than factual and obvious relationships. There is no limit to the possibilities of this approach.

The commercial or news photographer may ask now: "With five minutes allotted to taking my photograph, how in the world will I find time to make all these checks and evaluations?" The answer is simply this: the procedures outlined in this book are basic, and every photographer should *practice* them in order to perfect his craft. As his experience grows, such procedures become *automatic* for the most part; his arrangements, evaluations and conclusions can be effected rapidly. It is largely a conditioning of the mind to grasp and manage the technical and expressive problems with a minimum of delay. Reference is made to the musician; he practices in great detail and with great concentration. When he appears before his public he *commands* his medium. There is an old adage in music: "If you play when you practice, you practice when you play!" This is true in photography as well as in music! Some problems allow long and careful contemplation; others demand immediate solution. The greater the technical resource and understanding of the medium, the more perfect the intuitive response.

49. Theatrical Photograph, by Minor White. Here is a simulation of theatrical-lighting effect. It represents Mr. White's rare observance and exquisite technique. Mr. White says (in answer to request for information): "For data—the camera was faithfully used."

88

Many of the most expressive and powerful portraits have been produced with one or two lights alone. With "steady-burning" lights, we can see before us the effective balance of illumination, at least a balance acceptable to the eye. But with flashlamps the problems of portraiture become severe unless special illuminating accessories are used. A 2-circuit reflector unit (as described in Book 1, page 66) provides a solution to this problem under normal conditions. This device represents the simplest arrangement of the two circuits; it is obvious that far more elaborate units could be designed for special use and more precise controls. Many of the available speedlights have built-in "modeling" or "finding" lights. It is quite apparent to everyone, I am sure, that in using two or more of these 2-circuit reflectors we must be sure that the "steady-burning" lights (used as composing lights) are of the same intensity throughout, and the flashlamps used must likewise be of equal illumination output. Otherwise the balance of illumination adjusted to visual and exposure requirements will not be retained in the image.

The principle involved is simple: (1) the composing or "modeling" lights are so placed with regard to position and distance that the subject is revealed to the eye with the desired balance of lighting; (2) the relative brightnesses are adjusted to match the visualization requirements of the finished picture; (3) the known guide numbers for the flashlamps or speedlights employed are used to compute the lens stop and/or shutter speed setting. We assume that the guide number is based on the lamp and reflector used, film speed, shutter speed, and whatever factors are involved (see page 36). In working out the visualized image it may be necessary to make a considerable change in the distances of the lights from their optimum "visual" position. If the angle of light upon the subject remains the same, the modeling will remain practically the same, irrespective of moderate changes of distance. Of course, as the distance of the lights increases, both the shadow edge and the highlights become sharper.

The modeling lights need not be strong; in fact, the weaker the better, consistent with accurate appraisal of modeling effects. We must be sure to remember that when the level of illumination in the room is low, the pupils of the subject's eyes are *large;* this effect can sometimes be very unpleasant, and occasionally it will profoundly alter the expression of the subject. Thus the intensity of the modeling lights should be such as to create the impression of normal illumination— yet not strong enough to create effective images when the shutter is operated for the flash exposure. When working with synchronized flash and speedlight, the shutter speeds should be as short as possible to minimize any second lighting effect. By measuring the brightness of any area of the subject, we can determine what shutter speed (at a given lens stop) will be needed to place the values on or below the threshold of the negative. For example, using a film of Weston tungsten rating 32, a skin brightness from environmental lights or modeling lights of 1.6 c/ft^2 would require about 1/25 second exposure at f/5.6 to appear as a Zone I value in the negative—barely enough to affect the final image. Obviously, any exposure less than this would be of sub-threshold value. But if the modeling lights gave a brightness value of 6.5 c/ft^2, the negative, (exposed at about 1/25 second) would have a Zone III value and could produce an obvious secondary image. However, if the shutter were open only for 1/100 second or less, the values would then fall on or below the threshold. Synchronized shutter speeds of 1/25 second and faster at f/22 are quite safe in this respect unless the intrinsic subject-brightnesses are very high (or the subject is in motion). If the modeling lights are too bright, a slight movement of the head during the flash exposure might show a trailing catchlight in the eye.

Some Basic Lighting Plans

While it may appear a bit inconsistent to suggest "basic" lighting plans and setups after having depreciated lighting formulas, a few ideas on the subject may be helpful to those who have had no experience in lighting arrangements. These suggestions are only procedural sketches; each and every one may be modified to satisfy the individual problem at hand.

1. *First Steps:* Study your subject. Note values of skin, hair, clothing and background. Note qualities of skin—texture, blemishes, color. Note facial forms and expressions; almost every person has a "best" side, a most favorable position of the head and body. Be aware of long noses, jutting or receding chins, jowls, protruding ears. Visualize as best you can the appropriate quality of the image-to-be—contrast, balance of light and dark areas, separation of subject values from background values, etc. Avoid mergers of values unless you intentionally desire them. With a little practice you can conjure "mind's-eye" images which will help you tremendously when the actual setting up begins.

Needless to say, while the equipment used strongly influences your "seeing," there should not be rigid rules about the focal length of the lens used. The most accurate scale and proportion is, of course, achieved with moderately long-focus lenses, but a certain feeling of intimacy and proximity which the short-focus lenses give will be lacking. Short-, normal- and long-focus lenses all have their expressive uses. You may wish to emphasize facial form with exaggerated perspective by using short-focus lenses and working close to the subject.*

For most portrait work the author prefers a lens of *at least* 1.5x the diagonal of the negative. (The conventional norm is a focal length about equal to the diagonal of the negative—about 6½-inch focal length for a 4x5 negative.) Personally, a focal length of 135mm (about 5½ inches) for a 2¼x2¼ or 2¼x3¼-inch picture is ideal, but I have frequently used an 80mm or 75mm lens on negatives of these sizes with very good effect. The greater the lens-to-subject distance, the more favorable the depth-of-field effect; that is, more planes of the subject will be in good focus. For those who like eyes in focus, but nose and ears out of focus, the use of long-focus lenses and large apertures at close distances will do nicely! I prefer a reasonably sharp image throughout, with focus emphasis on the eyes. Beware of intrusively near hands, sleeves and shoulders. The position of the camera profoundly affects the aspect of the face; it is perhaps safe to say that a low camera position favors most men, and a normal or high camera position favors most women. Remember, if you do not observe the subject from about the same position of the lens, the picture will not represent what you "see." Hence the single-lens reflex camera is especially valuable for portraiture, except that in its

---

*It is assumed the reader knows that optical perspective depends entirely upon the distance of the lens from the subject; a 2-inch and a 20-inch lens give the same perspective at the same distance from the subject—but of course the image of the 20-inch lens is 10 times larger than that of the 2-inch lens. Using negatives of one size, on which are to be recorded images of the *same size*, we will find that as the focal length of the lens increases, we must *increase the lens-to-subject distance;* thus the perspective changes.

90

usual position the viewpoint is rather low. The new single-lens reflex miniature cameras with erecting pentaprisms have much to offer, for they operate at eye level.

2. *Backgrounds:* As a first experiment, place the subject against a simple background—say about 5 or 6 feet from a smooth wall. A light wall is preferred; if a very light background is required, the wall can be separately illuminated. If the wall is dark to begin with, it will be very difficult, if not impossible, to raise it to the proportionately high brightness value required. A light wall will probably reflect a middle gray value from the lights used on the subject unless the lights are too distant or directed away from the wall, or if the environmental illumination is weak. Background values depend entirely upon visualization and control of the subject-background tonal relationships.

3. *One-Light Technique (without reflecting screens):* After determining the best position of the subject before the lens, explore the best horizontal and vertical position of the light. In a large or dark room the shadows will be very deep— perhaps empty. If environmental reflections occur, shadows may have some tonal value which can be retained in the print. Note that the distance of the light from the subject modifies both the brightness and quality of shadow edge and highlights, and that the value of the environmental reflections may change little or not at all as the position of the light is changed. The farther the light from the subject, the less the brightness-range (subject contrast) ; this is because the environmental light value remains about the same, while the intensity of the direct light diminishes. If the environmental reflections are too high (that is, if at the best distance of the light from the subject, based on shadow edge and highlight quality, the subject contrast is not sufficient), the exposure can be reduced and development increased to achieve the desired opacity range in the negative (See Book 2). The selected position of the light will depend upon compositional factors, "modeling" factors, brightness-range factors, and possibly background requirements. Powerful portrait interpretations are possible with this extremely simple technique. To repeat, however: since the eye reacts to brightnesses quite differently than does the negative, it is important that the brightness values are accurately measured. As the majority of one-light pictures will be of basic high contrast, both shadowed and illuminated areas should be carefully metered so that undesirable empty shadows and "blocked" high values can be avoided, or at least controlled.

The single light placed near the lens axis will, of course, give a general illumination and the "limb" effect will be prominent (see page 24 and Book 4, page 8). In such conditions the background should be considerably lighter than the face so that the dark limb effect will be revealed most clearly. This demands not only a light wall, but a close proximity of the subject to the wall so that the single light on the subject will also illuminate the wall to the desired brightness value.*

---

*A typical situation might be as follows: Assume the single light illuminates a face to Zone VI value, and that the background is of an inherently high reflectance—in relation to the skin (35 per cent), it would reflect 90 per cent of the incident light. At the same distance from the light, skin would represent Zone VI, and the background Zone VII-VIII (a ratio of about 1 to 2½). Now, if the light were 4 feet from the subject and 7 feet from the background, the illumination ratio would be $4^2:7^2$ or 16:49—or about 1:3. As the background reflectance in relation to skin value is about 1:2½, we will see that the background will be only a little darker than the skin! However, the eye and mind, knowing the background is in itself lighter than skin, may not realize the actual luminous difference as the camera will see it! In such cases the only recourse is to add light on the background to adjust it to the desired value.

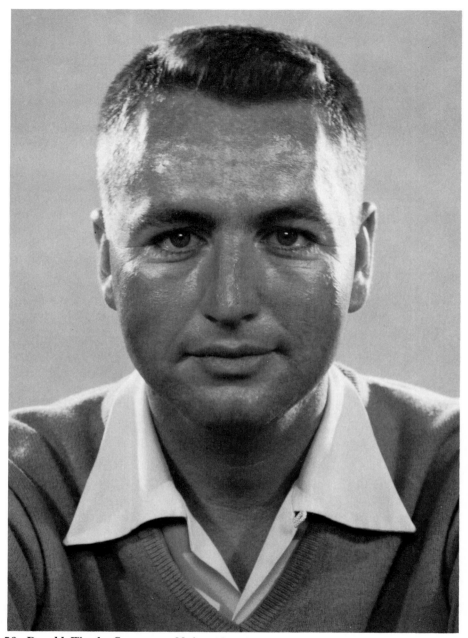

50. Donald Worth, Composer. Made with 4x5 view camera and 12-inch lens on experimental Polaroid Professional Panchromatic Land Film. This represents "core" lighting, using 2 lights positioned behind the subject and strongly lighting the sides of the face, with low-value light on the front (in this case coming from two small tungsten lamps). Note the "limb" effect, and the falling-off of light partially due to the inverse-square law effect. Actually, this subject was not ideal for "core" lighting; the face is a bit too full. The picture is shown to demonstrate that fact.

Shadows of the head on the wall should be avoided; therefore, not only should the light be very close to the lens axis, but it should be *behind* and slightly above the camera rather than on one side (shadows will then be smaller than the subject). Such lighting usually calls for normal-plus development, as the contrasts are chiefly those of the different reflective planes under equal illumination, and not the obvious contrasts of light and shade. And it is conceivable that such lighting—with the negatives developed to considerable contrast—might produce spectacular effects with a very dark background. Much depends, of course, upon the character of the subject. I believe that in such cases the head should be quite large in relation to the total area of the picture. This holds true in the majority of portraits against an extremely simple background of continuous tonality.

4. *One-Light Technique (with reflecting screens)*: The approach is the same as in (3) except that the reflecting screen offers a considerable control of shadow values. Obviously, the position of the screen relative to the position of the light is somewhat restricted. A diffuse reflecting screen is recommended because it will direct light onto the subject from various angles relative to the position of the main light, whereas a specular or semi-specular reflecting screen must be set to the angle of reflection of the main light. A specular or semi-specular reflecting screen will produce sharp secondary highlights and obvious "shadow-within-the-shadow," while a diffuse screen will provide illumination of a more "environmental" quality. The diffuse reflecting screen can be white fabric or cardboard, or a thin plywood or plastic board painted white. It can be supported by a folding stand and should be as large as is convenient to handle. It should be so positioned that the reflected light will strike the subject from the approximate level of the lens—neither too low nor too high. However, these effects, together with the general brightness effect, can be evaluated visually (although *accurate* brightness values should be checked with the exposure meter). As the main light and the reflecting screen illumination are usually directed at the subject from opposite sides of the lens axis, the position of the screen will exaggerate or minimize the "core" (see Fig. 50). Careful trials will determine the optimum position of the reflector. The brighter the reflected values, the more obvious will be the "core" at any reflector position. Remember, these effects can be appreciated by the eye, but seldom accurately evaluated visually in terms of actual brightness. This fact must be repeated because it is of the greatest importance for the beginner to recognize it. *Careful exploration by the exposure meter* will enable us to balance directly and indirectly illuminated areas, and the partially illuminated "core" area.

5. *Two-Light Technique (with or without reflecting screens)*: We will assume that the main light (such as used singly above) will first be employed to give the desired basic modeling of the face. The second light can be used as follows:

A. To illuminate the shadow area of the face directly, or by "bounce" technique.

B. To serve as a "decorative" light (background or top light).

If used as in (B), it will perhaps be necessary to employ a reflecting screen for proper illumination of the shadow areas of the face. In this case it will be found that the back or top light will often be in better position to illuminate the reflector than the main light. In all cases it is very important that the lens be entirely shielded from the direct rays of the lights by devices attached to the lights themselves (snoots, flags, etc.) and by an efficient lens hood as well. Whether or not the lens is

93

coated, *camera flare* can be damaging to the gradation of the image.

If the second light is used to illuminate the shadows, we can place it either at axis position or at any position away from the axis to produce the desired effect. At axis position we will find the "limb" effect most obvious with a light background, and there will be a definite falling off of the brightnesses of the receding planes of the face. The catchlights will be secured and the eye-socket illumination should be adequate. As we move the second light away from the lens axis position, secondary highlights and shadows will appear in the subject; and as the second light is moved farther from the lens axis, a strong "core" effect will appear. We must also watch for shadows on the background from the second light, especially when near the lens axis position.

Without doubt, "bounce" light (see page 43) is the best general method of using the second light. It has definite advantages over the ordinary reflecting screen receiving light from the main source, because it can be positioned independently of the main light or other lights used. If the "bounce" area is of high reflectant value, and all of the light from the second light in its reflector is concentrated on the bounce area, the actual light output can be within 20 or 30 per cent of that of the *direct* second light. And the quality of the bounced light is, to my mind, vastly superior.

To repeat, with modeling lights for flash it is important that all lights be of the same strength, although this is not imperative with steady-burning lights because the effective brightnesses of the subject can be metered and controlled. It is essential when "building" lighting for flash exposures that the modeling lights and

51. Graduation Photograph (courtesy, Dominican College of San Rafael). Made with Hasselblad Camera and 250mm lens. One Heiland IV Strobe on right. Shadows illuminated from second light "bounced" from screen. Some retouching needed on print to equalize complexion.

the flashlamps should each be consistent in their respective light output; that is, do *not* mix modeling lights of different power when lighting setups are being prepared and evaluated (unless the flash illumination is proportionate thereto).

The photographer will enjoy experimentation with the lighting setups as described. The use of more than 2 lights elaborates the problem, but gives more scope to imaginative visualizations.

6. *Multiple Lights:* Three light combinations include the main light, second light (direct or bounced) and decorative light, with or without reflecting screens. A 4-light combination might include the main light, second light, and 2 decorative lights, with or without reflecting screens. A 5-light combination might include the main light, second light, and 3 decorative lights (2 background lights and 1 top light, for example). Accessory lights can be used for the following special purposes:

A. Special lights to illuminate clothing, etc. (most useful in figure work).

B. Background illumination: the entire background can be brought to any desired brightness by the use of one or more lights. Variations of background tone can be achieved by judicious placing of the lights. If the background is of other than a continuous smooth surface—that is, if it is of recognizable objects and patterns—some difficult lighting and compositional problems may be encountered.

C. Special highlights: There can be achieved by a weak (say a 25-watt) lamp in or out of a reflector. Its light output can be sufficient to produce catchlights in the eyes and create some sparkle in jewelry, yet have no effect on the general illumination of the subject.

It is best to proceed with the applications of the different lighting setups outlined in this section; first as described, then perhaps by experimenting with supplementary lights—(A) (B) and (C) above. No two persons will approach the problems in the same way—and there is no reason why they should be expected to do so.

Problems of Color and Texture

Skin values include surface reflections (dry or oily qualities), general color (dark, tan, blond, or "peaches-and-cream" complexion), smooth or rugged textures, lines, lumps, under-eye pouches, good and bad teeth, and many other qualities that cause much trouble for all photographers. The few hints listed below may be helpful, but they cannot cover all the possible problems faced by the serious photographer.

A. *A dry "flat" skin* will stand "sharper" lighting than ordinary; highlights must be exaggerated. In extreme cases a slight application of face lotion will add vitality to the image, but it is best to avoid the obvious "cosmetic" or theatrical effects ("glamour" photography excepted!).

B. *An oily, shiny skin* usually requires softer and broader lighting than the ordinary; in extreme cases a light application of powder will be required. But again, be careful not to exaggerate the cosmetic effect.

C. *Freckles* are always troublesome. Use panchromatic film and a K2 filter, as most freckles are of yellowish or brownish color (they are seldom as dark as they look). With speedlights (usually of high color temperature, far more bluish than tungsten light) freckles and reddish or pinkish areas of the face may be rendered unpleasantly dark. Lips will also be rendered dark. A rather heavy yellow correcting filter is indicated. (The exposure factor with speedlamps, because of their high color temperature, would be greater than with tungsten lamps.) With panchromatic film and a K2 filter and tungsten illumination, such blemishes can be minimized, but red lips will perhaps be rendered too light. The only thing to do in this case is to apply a dark magenta color to the lips to assure their proper tonal rendition.

D. *Pink cheeks, etc.* These will cause some trouble; if the pinkish areas are rendered dark, the effect is one of gauntness and sallowness. If a yellow filter is used with panchromatic film, the entire face may become too light and "pasty." In such cases it is best to render the face rather smooth in tone, but use vigorous lighting effects to overcome the monotonous tonal values.

E. *Deep color and tone.* There is less reflectance difference than one might think between Negro and Caucasian skin; the highlight reflections are about the same, but the total effect of the first is one of considerable contrast. Average Negro skin is best placed, to my mind, on about Zone V of the exposure scale, and the skin of Orientals and tanned outdoor people can be placed somewhere between Zones V and VI. The "feeling" of skin color depends not so much on the actual brightness of the general reflectance of the skin, but on the contrast between these general areas and the highlight glare, as well as on textural quality.

F. *Texture.* Skin texture may be exaggerated or suppressed as desired by the quality and contrast of the lighting, filtering, degree of negative development, etc. It is quite obvious that much depends upon the character of the subject and the visualization of the photographer. Coarse textures are minimized by bounce light of relatively low value (image vitality can be retained by the use of top or back decorative light (see Fig. 13a). In this subject both strong textures and rugged lines have been minimized by the lighting described. On the other hand, a powerful rugged face may demand full textural and structural rendition.

G. *Evidences of ill-health or fatigue.* These can be very troublesome. They are difficult to overcome and are undeniably unpleasant to the eye in both the subject and in the photograph. Under-eye pouches, lines of strain, sagging features, etc., can be "managed" to a certain extent by lighting and some cosmetic treatment—but I frankly state that here is where retouching may be necessary. Best of all, wait for better conditions if possible!

H. *Teeth.* Most "toothy" mouths are difficult. If the usual expression reveals teeth, and if these teeth are uneven, overly large, in poor condition, etc., we must first adjust our lighting to minimize these effects. We must do all we can *before* exposure!

I. *Hand and face combinations.* There is no doubt that in many instances the organization of the hand with the face provides favorable solution to a variety of severe portraiture problems (see Fig. 19). Not only will the use of the hand cover a multitude of facial defects, but the combination of the hand and face may have esthetic connotations of real value. It is interesting to observe the differences of skin values of the face, palm and back of the hand. The texture of the ear is also quite different from that of the face, often appearing wax-like, and such differences seem more pronounced in the photograph than to the eye.

J. *Hair.* This is always a problem; do not confuse *sheen* with actual tonal values. Dark hair may photograph practically *black;* indication of its substance is often suggested only by its glistening highlights. Gray hair often photographs disappointingly drab—again, it is the visual impression of sheen that promises "high-key" images! The condition of the hair must also be observed; poor hairdressing, stray hairs, and too much hair lotion may appear surprisingly evident in the picture although barely noticed by the eye. With men, the condition of the beard is important; some subjects will need a close shave only a few hours before the sitting time. The photographer should train himself to look for all unfavorable aspects of the subject, and this includes clothing as well as the elements of face and form.

K. *Glasses.* Obviously, reflections in eyeglasses can cause serious difficulties, especially when the subject is illuminated with axis and near-axis lighting. The subject should be examined from a position as close to the axis of the lens as possible. Troublesome as it may be, removal of the lenses from the frames will simplify matters to a gratifying extent! However, there is sometimes danger here; certain types of eyeglasses demand very precise positioning in the frames. It would be better not to touch the lenses themselves, but to obtain an empty frame for the purpose. When sharp, angular lighting is employed, the shadows of the frames may cause confusing effects around the eyes. Whenever possible, photograph the subject without glasses; unfortunately, though, many persons always wear glasses and may appear self-conscious or uncomfortable—to say nothing of being unrecognizable!—without them. Reflections, on the other hand, may have great expressive value (see Fig. 48).

L. *Expression control.* A dangerous subject to discuss here. The techniques of establishing a good relaxed relationship between the photographer and subject demand much study. There is almost nothing worse than the imposed stereotyped expressions and poses that appear so frequently in professional portrait photography. Many subjects do show a desolate "freezing up" before the camera, and this is often evidenced by a hopeless mouth position; perhaps only under the camera do some persons become aware of their mouths! In such cases, the repetition of certain words—such as "beans," "prunes," "yes"—may induce relaxation of the mouth. In addition, the slightly ridiculous repetition of the words may amuse the subject and further serve to relax him. Music is sometimes, but not always, helpful. A calm mood in the photographer, and his suggestion that the subject think of things of some real significance to him, will induce a relaxed condition. Portraiture of all types depends upon the photographer's ability to catch the fleeting appropriate moment of expression—at least to *recognize* this moment as essential to the subject's character. It may seem out of place here to discuss expression and expression control, but it is important to realize that even a slight change of expression may suggest a change of lighting, not only because of altered configurations of the face, but because of a change in the mood and character of the subject.

Retouching

This is a subject which distresses many creative photographers. Actually, retouching need not mean *manipulation* of values and textures, even if it is practiced as such by a large number of professional portraitists. Retouching is really repair and the correction of defects. We "spot" our negatives and prints to remove pinholes, specks, scratches and other blemishes. If there is something in the image which *appears* as a blemish or a defect, there is no reason why it should not be eliminated by retouching means. The size of the image has much to do with the definition of "defect." Let us take the famous wart on Lincoln's cheek: in a large-scale portrait it appears as an important element in his physiognomy, and it would be entirely wrong to remove it from the image. But if a head is reduced to a considerable degree where a wart or other defect becomes unrecognizable as such, *appearing as just a small speck*, we might well be justified in removing it. The important decision lies in the distinction between *defects* and *details which are essential to character*. It has been my experience that if the subject accepts a realistic approach and if the tonalities and textures are treated in a forthright way, we are not conscious of facial details and defects nearly so much as when we attempt an "idealization" and, of course, fail.

Retouching is a highly specialized craft; when it is necessary, an expert should be retained for that purpose.

It is proper to mention here that many problems of difficult portraiture can be simplified by the use of the miniature camera ($2\frac{1}{4}$x$2\frac{1}{4}$ or smaller). The inherent image grain and optical limitations of the small image combine to produce a limited "covering" effect when it is enlarged to a moderate-to-great degree.

The reader may conclude that the art of portraiture is a difficult and rather mechanical procedure—what with all the recommended measures of light, the checks and counterchecks and attention to detail suggested above. However, we cannot discount experience; the more one works with light, the more familiar he becomes with the effects of light—just as a musician becomes familiar with his instrument and its complex, almost infinite harmonic and expressive possibilities. We must start at a point where we can grasp the simplest situations and command them. Then, as both our technique and awareness are sharpened, certain interrelations of values will assert themselves in our visualization; at this point we are forming our own personal approach. Soon technique and mechanical procedures become more or less automatic and *expression* takes over. We must constantly explore, discover, recognize and respond.

52. San Francisco Fire, April, 1906, by Arnold Genthe. This is a copy of a print from a Genthe negative, made on Polaroid Land Projection Film and engraved directly from the transparency image. The resolution of this material is very high and, in slide form, it projects with great clarity and brilliance. Refer to page 106 for remarks on copying transparencies.

53. Martha Graham in *Punch and the Judy* (a Dance Comedy) by Barbara Morgan. This is an excellent example of this great photographer's distinguished work in the field of the dance. The data: 3 No. 31 G-E Flashlamps; Speed Graphic Camera, 4x5; focal-plane shutter, 1/1000 second at f/16. The picture was made in the studio, not in stage performance. Barbara Morgan says: "I have bathed the composition in light by back-bouncing and top-lighting in order to do away with shadows—to make it seem an arena for folly and light-headedness. Shadows accompany bodies in a logical way—so it makes for the unexpected to do away with such logic in the setting. The rear horizon was carefully placed in the center of the revolving skirt—to make the violence of the skirt more inexorable." This represents a very advanced concept of planning and execution and demonstrates that if you know what you want, and have adequate technique (and experience!) you can achieve your objectives.

It is obvious that even with powerful photoflood illumination and films of the highest obtainable speed we cannot use really fast shutter speeds and arrest swift motion. With flashlamps, the duration of the flash is about 1/50 second. Shutters are synchronized to give short exposures within the "peak" of the flash. Special flashlamps of about 1/30-second peak duration are designed for focal-plane shutters. As the shutters, operating at relatively high speeds, use only part of the total output of the flashlamps, the effective illumination with the higher speeds is considerably reduced (in relation to the total output of the flashlamps on "open" flash shutter settings in which the entire light output of the flashlamps is used). Thus motion can be arrested with flashlamps using shutter speeds just as we would in daylight; but with daylight the light is constant, and we are not subject to the Inverse Square Law relating to light-to-subject distance.

With speed flash, the duration of exposure is the duration of the flash itself— from 1/500 to 1/30,000 second in commercially available models. As these speeds exceed the speed of mechanical shutters, the shutter can be operated at any speed. Focal-plane shutters cannot be used except at settings where the shutter is *completely* open during exposure (1/25 second with a Hasselblad, for instance).

However, should there be available light sufficiently intense to render an image (diffuse or specular) within the effective exposure produced by the shutter speed, we will have the combination of a sharp, fully arrested image of an object in motion (from the speedflash), and a "moved" image from the relatively slow shutter exposure.

What we term the "speed" of the speedlight relates to the duration of the *peak* of the flash. Most of the diffuse image brightnesses relate to this "peak" light. However, highly reflectant parts of the subject can pick up light from the beginning and end portions of the flash, and—since from the actual beginning to the actual end of the flash may represent only a few hundredths of a second—the specular reflecting areas may show motion while the diffuse reflecting areas will be entirely sharp! This phenomenon may appear when using two or more speedlights; one light used as a back light may produce a specular sheen on the hair or other elements of the subject, and this may show a little movement, while with the "front" light the motion of the subject in general is arrested, although both lights are firing simultaneously and at the same speed.

Unless we have speedlights of exceptional power, our sphere of activity is somewhat restricted and action will be limited to relatively close subjects. Esthetically, the complete "freezing" of the subject in motion may be questionable, especially in relation to portraits, but few can deny the tremendous importance of speedflash in almost every branch of photography.

An important element in action photography is the degree of movement of the *image on the film* in relation to the desired clarity at a given degree of enlargement. This movement across the film depends upon the angle of motion of the subject to the camera, the focal length of the lens, the distance of the subject and—as stated above—the desired degree of "arrested motion." The closer the moving object to the lens, the greater the movement across the film for any given exposure. Refer to the PHOTO-LAB-INDEX, Section 17, pages 24 and 25, for formulas and tables related to this subject. However, it is sometimes advisable to *show* movement when interpreting moving objects.

COPYING TECHNIQUES WITH ARTIFICIAL LIGHT

We should first define the term "copy." It is a simple matter to make a record picture of a painting, etching, photograph, map or other graphic object. However, if we wish to produce a copy of a photograph, for instance, which will approach in clarity, tonal range and esthetic effect the qualities of the original, we have set ourselves a major task. If we understand the practical procedures of the control of subject brightnesses, and exposure-development controls of the negative, we can be assured of considerable success. Printing is, of course, of extreme importance in terms of tonalities and "print color."

Equipment

The basic equipment is described in Book 1, page 70, and in Book 4, page 110, and will be adequate for most copy work of moderate size. With large paintings, screens, etc., the setup will naturally be more extensive. The principal requisites are ample space for the camera and the lights, and sufficient illumination for adequate and *even* lighting of the subject.

However, when working entirely with artificial light on such problems, some specific equipment may be necessary. Assuming that the photographer has all the needed filters, levels, focussing magnifiers, etc., it is suggested that he add a few helpful items such as the Kodak Pola-Lights, and, of course, a polarizer. These are very useful in removing sheen from the surface of prints and paintings, and minimizing or totally removing disturbing reflections from a great variety of subjects, thereby revealing textures and details otherwise submerged in glare. Of course, they must be used with great care and taste; many substances and surfaces are inherently highly reflectant, and we must not overdo the polarizing effect (see page 77 for description of the Pola-Lights and their general use).

Copying Photographs

We are all aware of the difficulty of making a truly satisfactory copy of a photograph. Paintings are easier to do because the results are *interpretive* in terms of black-and-white values, while the copy of the photograph demands a close *facsimile* quality. The nature of the characteristic curve of photographic materials tends to distort the scale of values of the subject, and this distortion is painfully apparent in the majority of ordinary copies of photographs. For a true rendition of values, all the values of the subject should fall upon the "straight-line" section of the characteristic curve of the copy negative. Theoretically, this copy negative should be developed to a gamma of 1.0. Then, printed on a paper of appropriate exposure scale, the print should duplicate the values of the original photograph. Unfortunately this ideal procedure does not always work out; in fact, it practically never does under ordinary circumstances of work. Some of the reasons are:

A. Environmental light (extraneous light in addition to the main illumination) may degrade the blacks of the subject and cast slight glare over the entire image. Reduce all extraneous (environmental) light to a minimum; it should not be more than 1/150 the intensity of the copying illumination. Check this as follows: place a gray card or a white card at the subject position and read the brightness value with the copying lights turned on. Then shield the card from the direct rays of the lights, and read the brightness value of the card as illuminated by the environmental light in the room. Remember that the copying lights will raise the general level of the environmental illumination (perhaps might be the principal cause of it), so a reading of the card brightness with the copying lights turned off would have little meaning. Obviously, a dark-walled, large room will produce a minimum of environmental light.

B. The copying lights may be at too acute an angle, thereby slightly degrading the whites; (minute textures in the paper—"hills and valleys"—will produce small shadows under low-angle lighting, thereby lowering the brightness value of the white areas). Also, watch for reflections. The copying lights should be at the optimum angle to the subject—that is, at the greatest angle consistent with complete lack of glare from the surface of the subject photographed. The only way to be certain that the angle of the lights is adequate is to examine the subject through the camera—not only on the ground glass, but with a direct view from the plane of the negative, having removed both lens and camera back (of course, the optimum viewpoint would be at the plane of the lens). The size of the subject being copied, the distance of the lens to subject, and the distance of lights from the subject, must all be taken into consideration. Normally two lights of equal intensity and distance will balance each other and minimize texture on the surface of the subject, but if the print is wrinkled or curled there may appear some obvious reflections.

Both lights must be at the proper distance to give *even* illumination. As noted on page 71 of Book 1, the axis of the lights should impinge a little beyond the center point of the subject. It is advisable to place a white card over the entire area of the copy subject and take brightness readings at various points on its surface, adjusting each light to assure consistent over-all brightness. When each light is so checked, turn on both lights and make a final check for perfectly even illumination.

C. Camera flare (and/or lens flare) will reduce the contrast of the image. It is quite important that the object copied be placed against a *dark* background and that all extraneous light be shielded from the lens. A lens hood that accurately cuts the field of view will help in this respect. We must remember that the lens "sees" a larger field of view than what is represented in the picture area, and that the image of this larger field will strike the interior of the bellows and reflect diffuse light onto the negative. Suppose we are copying a mounted print; the image of the print may fill the area of the negative, but the image of the white mount would be projected upon the bellows, and considerable flare would result. An adjustable lens hood (rectangular in form) is a very valuable accessory. When feasible, however, surround the picture being copied with black paper.

D. When copying subjects of highly reflective surface (such as a glossy print, or a print under glass) watch for possible reflections of the lens and front parts of the camera, and light objects near and behind the camera; these will frequently show in a continuous-tone area of the subject such as the sky. It is wise to have a large black card placed before the camera in which a hole has been cut to admit light to the lens. This serves in a way as a lens hood. In more or less permanent copying setups, the camera can be placed in a box, dead matte black inside and out, with an adjustable opening for the lens. This opening can be set to the same proportions as the picture being copied, and in that way practically all of the extraneous light is controlled. Also watch for reflections from the clothing of the operator and objects which might lie within the field of view.

E. The exposure may not "place" all of the values of the subject within the straight-line section of the characteristic curve; hence the image values may be distorted. There is no doubt that a slow "commercial" type of film (orthochromatic or panchromatic—the latter essential when the subject has color) possesses a more vigorous curve and greater opacity range and is therefore more suited to copying than the general-use film. However, standard emulsions such as Isopan, Panatomic-X, etc., can be used if the highest value of the subject is placed on Zone VII and normal-plus development is given the negative. This will require some personal testing for positive results.

If we analyze the brightness range of the average photographic print (a glossy full-tone image), we will find it about 1:50. The brightness range can be measured with the S.E.I. Meter under moderate illumination that is free from glare, and with no appreciable environmental light striking the print. If the lowest brightness is placed on Zone II, the highest value (the white of the paper) will fall between Zones VII and VIII. The lightest areas of the image will not exceed Zone VII, although the white paper base will be a little higher. As the whitest area of the *image* should be rendered as a Zone VIII in the copy *negative,* a normal-plus-1 development is needed. Since the white of the photographic paper is about the same as the white side of the Kodak Neutral Testing Card (90 per cent reflectance), the exposure can be determined by taking a reading from its surface (position at the subject) and placing its brightness value between Zones VII and VIII; then give normal-plus development. With tungsten light, of course, use the tungsten film-speed ratings. Also, do not fail to compensate for any lens extension, etc. A typical entry on the Exposure Record of a copy photograph might be:

Copy, *Portrait of X*
Film speed rating: ASA 64 (tungsten)
Lens: 14-inch Ektar, extended to 20 inches (exposure factor 2x)
Placements: in c/ft^2

	I	II	III	IV	V	VI	VII	VIII
White card								50
Gray card					10			
Lightest area of print.........							40	
Darkest area of print.........		1						

Basic exposure: 1/10 second at f/8
With ext. factor: 1/5 second at f/8
Actual exposure: 1 second at f/16 (precisely 4/5 second; but slight additional exposure justified by reciprocity effect (see page 4).

Development: Normal-plus-1

The above relates to ordinary tungsten lamps in appropriate reflectors. If the Pola-Lights and the polarizer are used, the basic exposure will be considerably greater (see page 79). First, adjust the circular screens before the light to normal —vertical—position (indicated by the arrows marked on them). Then view the illuminated subject through the polarizer. Select the angle of the polarizer at which all glare is reduced to optimum or disappears. Then take the brightness reading of the white card or the gray card with the meter, through the polarizer at optimum position, and calculate the exposure accordingly.

Complete polarization would obtain when the polarizer was at right angles to the polarizing axis of the Pola-Light screens, but this complete polarization may not be necessary or desirable in every case. The exposures are considerably increased with the use of the Pola-Lights and the polarizer, and there may be need for further increased exposure to compensate for the reciprocity effect (see page 4).

This reciprocity effect is actually beneficial to the scale of the copy negative; prolonged exposures (or exposures of very short duration) serve to lengthen effectively the straight-line portion of the characteristic curve. Speedlamps can be used with considerable success in copy work. Their high intensity and short duration make them especially efficient when making a number of copies in sequence. (Development of the negative will be about 2x normal.) Tests will be required for optimum results; we can start these tests by using the previously determined guide numbers (page 36) and "bracketing" the exposure through two lens stops above and below that one which is indicated by the guide number. A specific guide number can then be determined for copy work (in relation to the 2x normal development time). Do not forget to calculate for lens extension, etc., but in determining the final copy guide number, be sure it is a *basic* number and does not in itself include any other factors. If, for instance, the copy guide number was established for a 1.5 lens-extension factor, it would be incorrect for other extensions. The effectiveness of the speedlights when placed behind the Pola-Light screens, and with the polarizer at the lens, can be determined by interpolation. If, for example, the Pola-Lights and the polarizer combination increase the exposure 16x over what it would be with the same lamps and no polarizing equipment, then the exposure with speedlamps would be 16x that indicated by their guide numbers (plus extension factor, etc.). Obviously, we will have to use the regular lamps when setting up the Pola-Lights, but once the right polarizing combination is determined, we can position the speedlamps properly. Depending upon the design of the speedlamps, this may require some special attachments (a good camera mechanic should be consulted).

F. The printing paper may be of too long or too short exposure scale to reproduce properly the values of the negative. The exposure scale of the paper must relate to the opacity scale of the copy negative, just as with all other branches of practical photography. This relationship is even more critical because we are duplicating existing values and do not have the flexibility of personal tonal interpretation. No matter what negative material we use, I think it best to develop for a negative opacity range which will give a full-scale print on a No. 1 contact-type paper or a No. 2 projection-type paper. Small variations in the negative opacity scale can be compensated for by modifying the print exposure and development (see Book 3, *The Print*). Subsequent toning of the print is important, especially if the original is toned.

G. The printing paper used may not have a sufficiently brilliant surface; that is, the reflection-density (brilliancy) range may be inadequate in relation to that of the original photograph. On the other hand, if the original is a soft, low-brilliancy print, the paper on which the copy negative is printed should not have too brilliant a surface for proper interpretation of the original picture.

Whenever possible, slightly *reduce* the size of the copy below that of the original. This will minimize false textural effects, as well as an inevitable loss of definition. This loss of definition is really due to the fact that the paper, no matter how smooth or glossy, possesses some texture which is picked up in the copy image. There is also a slight "halo" in any negative or positive image, and this halo, when augmented by the second halo in the copy print, causes a slight apparent loss of definition. This is especially noticeable when the copy image is much larger than the original. When copying half-tone reproductions, it is always better to reduce to at least 2/3 the original size to minimize the screen effect.

When focussing the copy image, first compose and focus with the lens wide open; then stop the lens down and carefully *refocus*. This is not necessary with process-type lenses (which are especially made for close work), but standard lenses, being designed for different purposes, may show a change of focal position as the lens aperture is reduced.

Eastman Kodak Company produces a fine copy material — Kodak Gravure Copy Film — which has unique characteristics and capacities. As we know, one of the chief difficulties in making copies of continuous-tone images (such as a photographic print) lies in preserving the qualities of the whites. This new film is especially designed to retain accurate values in the higher tones of the original; both the subtle variations of tone in very light grays and the crispness of pure whites are properly interpreted. It is important to follow the instructions which Kodak gives for this material to achieve optimum results.

Copying Toned or Stained Photographs, etc.

In copying straight black-and-white prints, line drawings, etc., we may use ordinary "color-blind" or orthochromatic film, but if the image is on yellowish paper, toned sepia, etc., orthochromatic or panchromatic film is required (with "color-blind" film the yellowish paper would photograph gray). On the other hand, a sepia print, under tungsten light and with panchromatic film, might photograph too light—appear "washed out" in the higher values—as the yellow component of the sepia tone, plus the yellowish quality of the tungsten light, would tend to overexposure in general and, specifically, would merge the lighter values of the picture with the white paper base. A blue-green filter (Wratten No. 45) is helpful. An orange filter, (Wratten No. 15G) will minimize yellowish stains. Refer to Photo-Lab-Index, Section 20, for further data.

Copying Polaroid Land Prints

The Polaroid Corporation offers excellent copy service, but there are many occasions where the photographer will need to make his own copies of Polaroid Land prints. This print image usually reveals a full tonal scale and tolerates a high degree of illumination without losing the richness and solidity of the blacks. The techniques of copying photographs described in this section are applicable to the Polaroid Land images, except that consideration must be given to their relatively high contrast and glossy surface. Providing the optical image is adequate, the character of the Polaroid Land print will allow 2 to 2½x direct enlargement in the copy camera. The coating of the print must be even and free of dust specks, etc., which may show in the enlarged image. As with photographing any high-gloss surface, the front of the camera should be shielded with a dark card or cloth to prevent reflections showing in the image. As mentioned on page 101, the illumination on the subject should be about 150x greater than the "environmental" light in the room to prevent loss of brilliancy of the copy image.

The basic setup is quite different from that required for copying prints. The subject should be set in front of an illuminating box giving an even source of light. A cluster of lamps or a "cold-light" grid are advised for the illuminants. A sheet of opal glass should be placed between the transparency and the lights, sufficiently distant from the transparency so that no blemish or mark on its surface can be brought into focus when the lens is stopped down. The size of the opal glass and of the light-producing area should be considerably larger than the largest transparency to be photographed. The same principle applies to enlarging and is discussed in Book 3, page 34 (diagram on page 35).

The transparency should be matted down closely to the edges to prevent any stray light from coming through which might cause flare. If color copies are to be made of color transparencies, be certain that the light source is of standard color quality and that the color film used is balanced to the light. With black-and-white copies of color transparencies the nature of the light source is not so important. Most transparencies will be mounted between glass, or in plastic envelopes, and we must watch for reflections which could show in the dark areas of the subject. For best results, carefully remove transparency from glass or plastic sheaths. Therefore the room should be quite dark and the front of the camera shielded by the dark card mentioned on page 102 above.

Our exposure problems are quite different from those in copying prints. The contrast range of a negative or a lantern slide may be as high as about 1:100 (density range of 2.0), and that of a color transparency may be as high as 1:1000 (density range of 3.0). In copying black-and-white negatives, the same basic techniques as for transparencies are used, but we will usually wish to duplicate the opacity scale of the original (although we can make certain changes in that scale if desired. In any event, the S.E.I. Meter will be of great help; we can work very close and explore the extremes of brightness (or, to be exact, of density—opacity—although we figure these as brightness values in order to determine our exposure). In copying negatives, we will of course, get a positive. If we want a copy negative we can use the reversal film made especially for that purpose. This is a special technique, and adequate data are provided by the manufacturers.

If we desire a duplicate *negative* we have several ways of obtaining it:

A. We can make a fine print, and then make an accurate copy therefrom as described above. Of course, the negative relates to the *print* quality, and the tonal effects are restricted to those of this original print.

B. We can use the reversal film material, but the precision of the results in terms of really adequate duplication of values is questioned.

C. We can copy the negative—getting a positive—and then "print" the positive on another piece of film, or make a second copy. The "printing" technique will probably give the best results, since the second optical step is avoided.

D. We can use the Type 46 L Polaroid transparency material; this being a *positive* process, will yield a negative of high resolution and full scale. At present writing, the size is limited to $2\frac{7}{16}$ x $3\frac{1}{4}$ inches on 3 x 4 inch film, but there is no reason why moderate enlargements cannot be made with considerable success.

To return to the exposure problem, we have a rather large brightness scale to contend with in color transparencies, usually exceeding that of an average outdoor subject. We are not "interpreting" nature — we are trying to duplicate an existing scale of values. The distortions which the characteristic curve of the negative material possesses clearly indicate the need for a film of very long "straight-line" characteristics. The slow commercial orthochromatic (for black-and-white negatives) and panchromatic (for color transparencies) emulsions are best, but we must be careful not to overdevelop the negatives. Light of low intensity, requiring long exposures, will evoke the reciprocity effect and effectively lengthen the straight-line portion of the curve, but it will also increase the contrast of the image. Also, the lower the illumination *through* the transparency, the greater the effect of disturbing environmental reflections *on* the transparency. Thus the need for adequate shielding of the transparency from any extraneous light. The lowest densities of a transparency or negative approach zero (film-base-fog), and the highest densities may indicate a rather extreme range; we can control our copy image by changes of development time; the softer the original, the longer the developing time, and vice versa. The Zone System approach works very well here. However, since much of the charm of a transparency lies in the subtle and brilliant high values, any overexposure will tend to block out these subtle values. Hence they must not be overexposed (Zone VIII is the top limit for a texture of high value), and it is better as a rule to lose some texture in the lowest values rather than distort the highest values. The problem of copying a negative is almost the reverse of copying the positive transparency. The highest densities of the negative (representing the whites of the print) are the areas of lowest transmission brightness; they must be exposed so that subtle textures are preserved. The most transparent section of the negative (representing the shadow areas of the print) must also be exposed to preserve texture; too much exposure will "burn out" these subtle textures and the resulting image will be empty and blank.

Obviously, a very soft negative or a very contrasty negative will require special development. The basic exposure should, however, be planned so that the most opaque areas with texture and tonal modulation do not fall below Zone II. With a very soft negative, very full development (or the use of high-contrast film) is required. A slow, long-scale panchromatic emulsion (commercial panchromatic film), and a soft, shadow-favoring developer (D-23 and the 1 per cent Borax second bath) will probably be most effective (See Book 4, page 78, for description of the 2-solution developer, and page 8 herein.)

As a basis of experiment it is suggested that the brightness of the color transparency be placed on the exposure scale as follows:

Zone II: The most opaque area of the image (not the highest opacity of the film edge). We refer here to the darkest part of the image in which detail shows.

Zone VIII: The most transparent area of the image (not the clear film) in which some impression of tone and texture is apparent. Zone VIII is the ideal placement. But in actuality Zones IX and X or even higher will sometimes represent the high-value placement if the lowest value is placed on Zone II! Hence, in such cases the use of the 2-solution developer will have a very real value. Standard normal-minus-2 development will control the high values, but there may be a certain loss of vitality in the lowest values. A smooth progression of tones is the prime objective. I have had very good results with Kodak Royal Pan, developing for 2x normal time in DK-50 for ordinary copies, and developing in the 2-solution formula (see page 8) for high-contrast transparencies. An important technique which is invaluable in controlling extremes of contrast involves the use of "masks."

Masking methods, used mainly for softening the extreme color contrast of a color transparency when making separation negatives, are described in the PHOTO-LAB-INDEX, pages 16-18 to 16-89 inclusive. The same methods may be used to make a low-contrast black-and-white copy negative from a color transparency or a low-contrast print from a contrasty negative; in the latter case, filtering the mask exposure is unnecessary and the mask may be made by white light.

A more complex method sometimes used in black-and-white work for exaggerating the contrast of both highlights and shadows, while depressing the contrast of middle tones, is known as the Person Process. A short description of this procedure will be found in *Enlarging*, by C. I. Jacobson, Focal Press, London, 1948, pages 209 and 254.

When copying a color transparency on black-and-white film we are confronted with the same problems of color rendition as when photographing the actual scene or subject, except that the colors of the transparency will usually have a higher saturation (that is, the colors are more brilliant) than those of most objects in the world about us. The Wratten Stereo-Green Filter (No. 55) is excellent in balancing the entire color range (lowering the blues and reds in value and raising the greens). With panchromatic film without a filter, reds are rendered rather light (especially with tungsten light) and greens lower in value than the eye sees them. Hence the fine compensating value of the No. 55 filter. On the other hand, to achieve the desired emotional effects we may use yellow, blue or red filters just as we do in landscapes, etc. The higher the color saturation, the more effective the color filters will be; therefore we will probably use weaker filters than when photographing nature (a K1 rather than a K2, a G or E rather than an A, etc.)

The making of lantern slides (regular or 35mm) is a special technique, and there is a large fund of information available on it.

Copying Paintings

The prime prerequisites of the setup for copying paintings are somewhat similar to those for copying photographs. These points should be considered:

A. The surface of the painting must be *evenly* illuminated, and no glare from the lights should show when the subject is viewed from camera position. This problem of even illumination is often troublesome; the eye may not appreciate slight variations in brightness, but these variations may be distressingly obvious in the finished picture. The consistent illumination can be tested by reading the brightnesses of a gray or white card placed at various positions over the surface of the subject. With a small painting the problem is minor. With a large painting we can meet with a lot of trouble. The lights must be placed at a distance sufficiently great to overcome obvious inverse square illumination loss from one side of the picture to the other. It is true that when two lights are used, one light will balance the other to a certain extent, but the adjustment of the lights must be quite precise —both as to equal distance and to illuminating angle. Watch for shadows projected on the painting from the frame. With a deep frame, removal of the painting therefrom may be necessary.

B. Be certain to check the precision of the setup; the painting must be parallel to the focal plane of the camera, *both horizontally and vertically*. There is nothing so suggestive of carelessness as a copy negative which is non-rectilinear. It is always helpful to have accurate parallel lines etched on the focussing screen to assure a truly rectilinear image. The camera should be centered and the focus carefully checked corner to corner. A small white calling card is an excellent "target" for accurate focus (but do not forget to remove the card before exposure!) If a large painting is installed in a home or museum, and is difficult to move to a more favorable location for photographing, we must make the best of the situation. If the painting is hung at an angle from the wall, the camera back must be set parallel to this position; a small protractor level is very useful here. With it the angle of the painting and the angle of both the back and lens board of the camera can be quickly matched. If windows, lighting fixtures, etc., cause unwanted reflections, they must be overcome by shielding. Environmental light on paintings can cause troublesome glare and distortion of values, especially in the darker areas.

C. Whenever possible the painting should be photographed against a dark background (see C, page 102). Flare of all types is harmful to painting copy images, just as with copies of photographs.

D. Surface reflections (often very complex because of the texture of the paint itself and the addition of varnish to the painting surface) can be controlled by the use of Pola-Lights and a polarizer over the lens (follow the same procedure as in copying photographs). See pages 77 and 104.

E. Panchromatic film is required, and filters will frequently be necessary to control color values properly (refer to Book 4, page 110, for a discussion on the use of filters). In this respect, approximately the same filters as used for copying with natural light can be applied, but with certain modifications if tungsten lighting is used. Filters and the polarizer can, of course, be used together with proper exposure factors applied. The Wratten Stereo-Green, No. 55, is an excellent filter for general use.

F. If the painting is covered with glass, reflections may cause trouble. Every effort must be made to eliminate environmental reflections, reflections of the camera, lens, operator, etc., in the glass. It will be well to cover the entire camera with a black cloth, or shield it with a large black card, leaving as small an opening as possible for the lens. The brightness from environmental light should not exceed 1/150 the brightness from the main illumination.

G. Exposures should be adequate to give "body" to the deepest values; these values are somewhat different from the blacks of the photographic print. They represent the physical "substance" of the pigment, and this should be suggested in the copy image. Brush marks, heavy paint deposits, etc., are all part of the structure of a painting, and both lighting and exposure must be adjusted to reveal, but not necessarily exaggerate them.

H. A painting, because of its color, may appear more contrasty than it actually is; viewing through a monochromatic filter (such as a Wratten No. 90 viewing filter or a rather heavy neutral-density filter) will give a better impression of its actual brightness scale. However, a copy of a painting is more an interpretation than a mere photometric duplication of values, and in black-and-white photography we can approach a painting somewhat as we would an object of nature. (A color copy, however, involves some rather complicated techniques.)

Exposure can be determined by placing the brightness reading of the gray card on Zone V, or the brightness of the white card between Zones VII and VIII. The actual brightnesses of the painting can be read with the S.E.I. Meter, but if the colors are of high saturation this may be difficult.

Copying paintings with available light only may be necessary at times. Here we have a problem of existing imperfections due to environmental light (which probably will reduce the over-all contrast of the subject), glare from unmanageable light sources, etc. If we cannot control these defects we must make the best of them. Exposure will usually be less than normal with appropriate normal-plus development. Some manipulation of the developed negative and of the print may be necessary. It will be found that the use of a very long-focus lens—as long a focal length as can be applied in the available space—will minimize the surface glare on the painting simply because of the angle of view, and therefore the number of sources of possible reflections is reduced. Also, the use of a long-focus lens will minimize rectilinear distortion.

Copying Daguerreotypes

Due to the high specular and low diffuse reflectance of the daguerreotype image we must prepare a special setup, as follows:

The direct light on the subject must be at an angle which will preclude any direct reflection whatever. The direct light must be sufficiently intense to overcome completely the effect of environmental reflections. The camera lens should be recessed behind an opening in a black-surfaced box so that a minimum amount of extraneous light will impinge upon the lens. The front of this box should be painted a dead black and be large enough to serve as a screen which will prevent environmental light reaching the daguerreotype. Should there be any reflection whatever of the lens and shutter, the daguerreotype can be tilted from the perpendicular, and the camera back and lens board likewise tilted to correspond. This will preserve the rectangular image, but change the angle of reflection.

Daguerreotypes are of low actual brightness range; a "duplication" of values in a photographic print is not feasible. The print image should be rich and full-scale. This means that the deepest values of the daguerreotype should be placed on Zone II, and up to 2x normal development given the negative. The best way to determine the brightness value is to take a reading with the S.E.I. Meter *through* the camera (with back and lens removed). The tonal quality of the copy print should convey the richness and delicacy of the original; it is suggested that the print be toned in selenium to a slight degree of cool purple-brown.

Copying Etchings, Lithographs, Drawings

The technique for copying these subjects is about the same as for copying photographs and paintings. However, to retain full textural values of the papers on which these images appear, placement of the brightness of the paper base should not be higher than Zone VII, and sometimes Zone VI (with considerably prolonged development of the negative). If we desire just a record of "line," we can use high-contrast materials and get a bold, highly exaggerated image. But if we want more or less facsimile reproduction, we must consider the quality and texture of the paper on which the original appears. Too much exposure will result in a loss of crispness in the delicate lines (largely due to inter-emulsion flare) and the "blocking up" of the paper texture. If the exposure is too short, the paper texture may appear exaggerated and the lines too harsh, even with prolonged development. The angle of illumination should be such as to avoid exaggeration of paper texture, wrinkles, etc. High contrast accents uneven values of thin lines on rough paper.

54. Copy of Daguerreotype. This copy was made on experimental Polaroid Panchromatic Land Film with the Kodak Master View Camera, and the engraving made direct from the original print. The camera front was shielded with a large black cardboard, and all reflections from the Daguerreotype and its glass cover were effectively eliminated by reducing environmental light, as discussed on page 101, and strongly illuminating the subject with two balanced lights set at a non-glare angle. Pola-Lights and polarizers will have some effect on metallic scratches etc., but it is advisable to rotate the Daguerreotype from vertical to horizontal position and select the position in which such defects are at minimum. The cleaning of Daguerreotypes is a tricky and hazardous operation; a new method is presented in *Image* (the Journal of Photography and Motion Pictures of the George Eastman House, Rochester, N. Y.), Vol. 5, No. 7, Sept. 1956, "An Improved Method for the Restoration of Daguerreotypes," by Charles van Ravenswaay, Missouri Historical Society.

When copying or photographing small objects, the camera front may be in a relatively difficult position for easy examination, and setting of lens stops and shutter speeds becomes a problem. The use of a concave shaving mirror helps facilitate seeing, and setting the shutter.

A pencil drawing is perhaps the most difficult to copy; not only are the lines faint and of delicate values and widths, but the lead will sometimes produce a sheen which at certain angles to the light can weaken the lines to the point of extinction. The Pola-Lights with polarizer will help to clarify such images. Paper-base brightness should not be placed higher than Zone VII (preferably between Zones VI and VII), and development should be about 1½x normal. Delicate aqua tones, water colors, etc., are difficult chiefly because of their subtle colors. Color filters must be used judiciously.

Copying Line Drawings, Maps, Typography, Etc.

For these subjects, special high-contrast materials will give the best practical results (process film, color-blind, ortho or panchromatic, depending upon the colors of the originals). Except in rare instances the texture of the paper is not important; we desire bold and sharp images against a white background.

However, ordinary negative materials can be used if properly exposed and developed. It is suggested that the white card brightness be placed on Zone VI and that at least 2x normal development be given the negative. However, this will result in negative grain in small negatives which will be obvious in subsequent enlargements. With 4x5 negatives (to be enlarged, say, to 8x10) the grain should not be troublesome, especially if a fine-grain film such as Panatomic-X is used. The low placement of the white paper on the exposure scale minimizes inter-emulsion flare and the delineation will be crisp. If the negative grain is troublesome, it will be well to expose as indicated above, but to develop only to normal-plus degree; the use of a printing paper of higher contrast will provide the required image contrast.

Photographing Sculpture, Metals, Etc.

In Figure 39a, page 72 the reflections of skylight and of a fixed lamp produce a complexity of reflections which do not relate to the form of the object. In Fig. 39b the reflections of the fixed lamp have been removed, and it will be seen that the reflections from the skylight alone suggest the quality of the surface to an adequate degree. The general illumination of the figure is from the environmental light in the museum gallery. Water-bath development was used to amplify the values of the lower and middle tones.

Figure 55 ("Oriental Stone Sculpture") shows the use of "bounce" light, plus a small amount of direct light to create some highlights. When photographed in direct light, the contrasts were too severe and the character of the material exaggerated, although a more dramatic effect was obtained. The *function* of the photograph must be taken into consideration; "museum" photography favors a complete rendition of detail and values for study and reproductions, but with "expressive" photography we can take some liberties with interpretation. Yet there should always be a controlling respect for the subject as a work of art.

In photography of polished metals, one method of early days was to rub putty or scatter talc or magnesium powder over the surfaces to "kill" the reflections. The result was that polished silver looked like plaster of paris or putty, and air-brush work was necessary to "create" highlights and intensify form. Another method was to enclose the polished surfaces in a "tent" of thin fabric; directing light on the outside of the tent produced a very diffuse illumination. But of course all of the surfaces would reflect the illuminated cloth, and an effect somewhat

55. Oriental Stone Sculpture, photo by Pirkle Jones and William Quandt (courtesy, M. H. de Young Memorial Museum, San Francisco). A combination of "bounce" light and some direct light for highlight accent. In images such as this, where values are "quiet" and full detail and texture preserved, the negative can be given Normal-plus-1 development and the textures "expanded" without losing detail in high or low values; or a more contrasty printing paper can be used. The integrity of form and substance must be retained.

similar to the putty-powder technique was obtained. A third method, giving a similar effect, was to paint with light from a large card or screen suitably illuminated from a properly placed light source.

We must remember that polished metals such as silver, chromium, etc., are almost completely black, except when reflecting light sources or illuminated objects. They have little or no capacity to reflect diffuse light. The essence of their quality lies in their reflections. A polished silver sphere suspended in a totally black environment would show only a single sharp reflection of a spotlight turned upon it. A broad floodlight would show a single but larger area of reflection. A white rectangle would appear as a curved white form, etc. In such cases, an environment of smooth material of a brightness level which would reflect about a Zone III or IV value on the sphere would provide a good basic tone. And a sharp highlight would complete the realistic effect.

Conclusion

Many minor procedures cannot be discussed here, but they will occur to the photographer as he explores the general copying techniques. The making of lantern slides and microfilm photography is worthy of much research and experimentation.

A word about lenses for copying: The ideal lens for close-up work is a process-type lens (that is, a lens especially designed for highest quality images when working within distances up to several times the focal length of the lens). However, for all practical purposes a fine anastigmat will serve the purpose admirably. But for very close work (obtaining images of equal, or nearly equal size) the process-type lens has decided advantages. A good focussing magnifier is essential, and with subjects that are not sharp in themselves, focussing can be determined from a calling card or other small area containing sharp lines or characters, placed *flush* with the surface of the subject.

Filters should be of high quality. The larger the image, and the longer the focal length of the lens, the more exacting the optical qualities of the filters must be. A-glass filters (optical flats) are very expensive, require careful orientation (when used in sequence), and are subject to serious damage if handled roughly, dropped, etc. Gelatin foils are cheaper, and perform excellently in practical photography.

Important! The camera and the subject must be placed and supported so that no vibration or movement of any kind is possible. The exposures will sometimes be rather long, and walking about may jar the floor and the camera.

Example of Lens-Extension Table

When the lens is extended beyond its normal "infinity" focus position, the relative values of the stops are reduced, and exposure must be increased accordingly (see page viii for description and formula). In copying, the lens is extended to varying degree, depending upon the subject-image size ratio. It will save much time if exposure-factor tables are prepared for the lenses used in copy work. For example, with an 8-inch lens:

Lens Extension	Approx. Exp. Factor	Lens Extension	Approx. Exp. Factor
9	1.25	14	3
10	1.5	15	3.5
11	2	16	4
12	2.25	17	4.5
13	2.6	18	5

114

115